Copyright © 1975 David Brown

First published in 1975 by
Macdonald and Jane's
Macdonald & Co. (Publishers) Limited
St. Giles House, 49-50 Poland Street,
London W1A 2LG

Made and Printed in Great Britain by
Morrison & Gibb Ltd
London and Edinburgh

ISBN 0 356 08095 1

Layout and Make-up: Michael Jarvis
Maps: Peter Sarson and Tony Bryan
Fighter profiles and Diagrams: P. Endsleigh Castle

D1642260

Contemporary Fleet Fighters: (*early 1930's*)

Above. Nakajima A4N-1 fighters (foreground) run up prior to take-off from the Imperial Japanese Navy carrier *Kaga*.

Immediately behind the fighters are a dozen Aichi D1A1 dive-bombers, with at least 18 Yokosuka B4Y torpedo-bombers behind them. (*Motoyoshi Hori*)

Below, left. A Hawker Nimrod Mark II over the patchwork of the English countryside. Built in late 1935, this model was capable of 195 mph at 14,000 feet. (*IWM MH28*)

Below, right. Boeing F4B-2 of VF-5B lands aboard USS *Saratoga* with a damaged starboard wingtip. Note the under-wing bomb racks and the 50 (US) gallon jettisonable 'slipper' fuel tank. (*USN 80-CF-54854-1*)

CARRIER FIGHTERS

CARRIER FIGHTERS 1939-1945
David Brown

Macdonald and Jane's: London

Contents

1. Introduction

The naval fighter aircraft's prime purpose is to defend the Fleet against air attack. Once the security of its 'base' is assured, it can then turn to the offensive. To achieve ascendancy in the air, the fighter must be able to find, catch, and destroy enemy aircraft. It must therefore be able to detect the enemy, or be assisted to do so, it must have the performance to enable it to reach a position from which an adequate armament can be brought to bear on the target, and the pilot must have the training to enable him to hit the target.

Prior to the Second World War, there were two principal classes of fighter aircraft. The most common was the 'interceptor', a primarily defensive fighter tasked with intercepting reconnaissance or bombing aircraft relatively close to its own base. Sufficient fuel was carried to make the interception, carry out attacks until the ammunition was exhausted, and return to base with a small reserve of fuel. Usually the smallest class of combat aircraft of its day, the interceptor combined the minimum airframe weight with the maximum available engine power; it was therefore invariably a single-engined, single-seat fighter – such as the Supermarine Spitfire, Messerschmitt Bf 109, or Morane-Saulnier MS.406. American Army Air Corps fighters such as the Curtiss P-40 and Bell P-39 Airacobra had an important ground-attack role in addition to any interception capability, and these fighters were designed to meet rather different requirements.

The second class of fighter was the long-range fighter, intended to escort bomber formations. Two engines were needed to supply the power to haul the extra fuel and the second (or even third) crew member who navigated and/or operated the wireless (W/T) set. Typical of the breed were the Messerschmitt Bf 110 and the French Potez 630 series; the Lockheed P-38 Lightning was untypical in that it was a single-seater. In each case, the twin-engined fighter possessed a top speed comparable to that of its single-engined stablemate, but its greater size and weight made it far less manoeuvrable. Paradoxically, the long-range fighter was usually the better bomber destroyer, while the single-seat interceptor was suited to the general air superiority role.

The navies which operated fighters from carriers could not afford the luxury of two classes of fighter. The limited space for stowage and the minimum maintenance equipment aboard ship make diversity of types undesirable: ideally, an aircraft carrier would be most efficient if only one type of aircraft, of one model or Mark, was carried. Maintenance and servicing, storage of spares, movement of aircraft on deck, and control of the flying circuit, all would be simplified and result in higher aircraft availability. As no nation's aircraft industry has yet been able to design an aircraft which can fulfil all the combat roles demanded of naval aircraft, the nearest approach to the ideal has to be the reduction of the number of separate types carried to a minimum – one fighter and one or two strike/patrol types.

The carrier fighter must therefore be a general-purpose aircraft, capable of defending the Fleet and of undertaking strike escort duties out to the maximum radius of action of the strike aircraft embarked in the same ship. To fulfil these requirements, it must be able to engage any potential enemy aircraft on favourable terms, combining the speed and manoeuvrability of the land-based interceptor with the long range of the twin-engined fighter.

But there are environmental requirements which affect the design of shipboard aircraft and impose severe restrictions on the basic size and weight. Size is dictated by the dimensions of shipboard features such as the width and length of the flight deck, the dimensions of the lifts between the flight deck and hangars, and of the hangars themselves. Although wings and fuselage extremities can be folded to reduce the aircraft's 'volume' for stowage, they must still be spread prior to launch, and the larger the size of the spread aircraft, the fewer that can be 'ranged' on deck at one time. Weight limitations are imposed by the strength of the decks and lift platform, and by the capacity of catapults, arrester wires and safety barriers. A major warship has a service life of about 25 years, following a design and building period of at least five years. The naval architects and constructors, advised by aviation experts, must design a ship which will be able to operate a generation of aircraft entering service 25 years later. New flight deck machinery must fit within existing physical dimensions but can only be incorporated in the course of highly expensive modernisation programmes, which keep the ship out of service for long periods. In general, the 'generation gap' between machinery improvements is greater than that between successive aircraft designs, so that the aircraft must always be tailored to suit the carrier.

The main enemy of the naval fighter is therefore weight, but the need for greater fuel capacity and the strengthening of the airframe for deck operations both tend to push the design to the limit. Internal tankage is usually greater than in land-based contemporaries, but this is still further increased by adding external jettisonable fuel in 'drop tanks'. Discarded in combat, the tanks give the aircraft the virtue of extended range without any penalty of weight and drag in an emergency. The basic structural weight remains, however. The aircraft must be strong enough to absorb the fore-and-aft loads imposed by the catapult – a loading unknown to the designer of land-based interceptors – and the fuselage bending loads imposed in landing at a 50 per cent higher vertical velocity than on an airfield. Local strengthening is needed around the arrester hook, catapult attachments and the undercarriage, which must itself be stronger than that fitted to a land-based aircraft of comparable weight. Such strength cannot be obtained without penalty – the Seafire Mark IIC was 800 lb heavier than the Spitfire Vc from which it was adapted – a 13 per cent increase in empty weight incurred by 'navalisation' to produce a fighter whose fragility at sea was a byword.

Fortunately, the wing-folding feature allows the naval fighter to be slightly larger than a shore-based interceptor, so that the greater wing area compensates for the extra weight, on take-off and when climbing or manoeuvring. Aerodynamic devices to reduce stalling speed and improve low-speed flying qualities during take-off or landing are essential for naval aircraft – the British Fairey Flycatcher fighter introduced landing flaps to naval aviation as early as 1923, and the American Grumman F11F-1 Tiger of 1957 was the first production aircraft to feature boundary layer control – 'blown flaps'.

The greater weight and size usually result in a slightly reduced maximum speed by comparison with a similarly-powered land-based interceptor. On the other hand, the latter cannot approach the carrier fighter for versatility of role and flexibility in operation. In 1940, the Blackburn Skua could fly a defensive patrol over the Fleet and on its next sortie be used as a highly-effective dive-bomber; by 1944, the Grumman Hellcat was flying air superiority missions over enemy airfields, as well as running up prodigious scores against Japanese attack aircraft, and today the McDonnell-Dougles F-4 Phantom is the best general-purpose fighter and strike aircraft in the Free World.

Fleet Defence

The aerial threats to the Fleet are posed by the enemy's long-range reconnaissance aircraft and attack aircraft. As early as 1914, scouting Zeppelins followed and reported the movements of the British warships in the North Sea, and in spite of many attempts to get fighters to sea, it was not until August 1916 that a Bristol Scout took off from a flying-off platform over the bows of the seaplane carrier HMS *Vindex* to drive off a Zeppelin. A year later, on 21st August 1917, Flight Sub-Lieutenant B. A. Smart, RN Air Service, took off from a light cruiser's platform and destroyed the German Navy Zeppelin *L.53* – the first 'kill' by a shipborne fighter aircraft.

The airship possessed the attribute of great range and endurance. Once it had found the enemy, it could remain in touch, reporting the movements of the ships until driven away or forced to return to base due to lack of fuel. Not until late in the First World War did heavier-than-air craft enter service with sufficient fuel to take over the 'shadowing' role. Smaller and faster than the airship, the aircraft was less vulnerable to interception, and it was a smaller target for the ships' improvised anti-aircraft armament and rudimentary fire-control. Unless driven away, the shadower could summon up attacking forces – submarines, surface warships, or aircraft. It was therefore essential to the safety of the Fleet that such reconnaissance aircraft should be destroyed or driven away as soon as possible.

By 1939, the range of options open to air forces wishing to attack ships at sea consisted of bombing from medium heights – level bombing, of releasing a bomb in a dive at low altitude – dive-bombing, or attacking with a torpedo. The first was the most attractive to most land-based air

An early attempt to find the answer to the Zeppelin – a Sopwith Schneider (left) and a Sopwith Baby (with unsynchronised Lewis gun) embarked on HM Submarine *E-22*, in May 1915. To float the aircraft off the submarine needed only to trim down. (*MoD(N)*)

The easier answer – a Sopwith Pup takes off from a 20-feet platform built over the tail of one of the battlecruiser HMS *Repulse*'s 15 in gun turrets. (*IWM Q65580*)

forces: the aircrews were already trained in this form of delivery against land targets and no specialised aircraft was needed. Mathematically, it was a sound form of attack: a formation of bombers, releasing a given number of bombs, would lay a pattern of bombs across a target. The tighter the formation and the larger the number of bombs dropped, the better the chances of a hit from the pattern. It was unfortunate for the bombers that actual circumstances had more influence than mathematical probabilities: navigation over the sea required specialised training, as did the recognition of warships and estimation of their course and speed. Wind speed and direction also exerted their influence – the penalty for a 5-knot error in estimated wind (or target) speed was 25 yards for every 10 seconds of the bomb's fall. With bombs taking up to 30 seconds to descend from 15,000 feet, the target had ample time to take evasive action to turn away from the estimated point of impact.

Dive-bombing had the advantage that the time of flight of the bomb was short, and that the pilot of the attacking aircraft, tracking the ship through his sight during the dive, was able to make more accurate allowances for target and wind speed and direction. The one heavy bomb of the dive-bomber was therefore likely to fall closer to the desired impact point than the many lighter bombs of the level bomber. By delivering a co-ordinated attack, from several directions at once, in a short but concentrated stream, the dive-bomber force could saturate the ships' AA defence organisation. Although the Luftwaffe's Junkers Ju 87 'Stuka' was to become the man-in-the-street's idea of the typical dive-bomber, it was the US Navy which had developed the type as a ship-sinking precision weapon, and that service and the Imperial Japanese Navy were to take the dive-bomber to its ultimate pitch of efficiency.

The third major means of delivering a weapon against a ship was the torpedo-bomber. Torpedoes, striking below the waterline and causing extensive flooding damage, carry more explosive in relation to their weight than an equivalent weight of armour-piercing bombs. In addition to the flooding, they inflict considerable shock damage to optical, mechanical and electrical systems throughout the ship. The ideal anti-warship weapon, it was also the most difficult airborne weapon to launch accurately. The gyros which control depth-keeping and maintain the desired course in the water are delicate instruments which have to be protected from excessive shock on entry into the water, and so maximum height and speed at release from an aircraft had to be limited – to about 300 feet and 250 knots in the case of the robust Japanese Type 91 torpedo and 100 feet and 120 knots in the case of the fragile US Mark XIII Bliss-Leavitt 21 in torpedo. The angle of entry was also critical – if too shallow then the torpedo would suffer damage, if too steep then it would never take up the correct running depth, even if it did not go straight to the bottom.

Because the torpedo had a relatively slow speed in water, considerable allowance had to be made for the target's movements, including possible evasive action, and a single torpedo-bomber had little chance of success against an alert target. Co-ordinated attacks, by as many aircraft as possible, releasing torpedoes on many bearings as near simultaneously as possible, were very difficult to counter. Executed as a well-rehearsed set-piece, in combination with dive-bombers, the torpedo attack was the most

The lethal torpedo-bomber – a 'Jill' bores in on USS *Yorktown* in spite of heavy AA fire. (*US Navy*)

serious threat to any form of shipping.

The price of failure was almost invariably higher for the defenders of shipping than for the defenders of land targets. Until 6th August 1945, a bomb hit on a city might cause considerable damage and heavy loss of life, but London, Berlin and Tokyo continued to function as centres of production and administration even after many thousands of tons of bombs had been dropped on them. By contrast, a single bomb or torpedo hit on a warship could seriously impair its fighting efficiency, leaving it vulnerable to follow-up attacks if it did not sink it outright. The guns' crews and fighter pilots defending the ships were *personally* affected by the fate of the target.

In reply to the various forms of air attack, the ship at sea was considerably helped by its relatively small size and its ability to manoeuvre. Long-range AA gunfire could provide a defensive barrage out to about eight miles and up to 20,000 feet, while ever-increasing numbers of close-range automatic AA guns provided a formidable defence against torpedo-bombers out to 4,000 yards and up to 5,000 feet. Well-directed long-range AA gunnery could disrupt bomber formations and close-range fire could force aircraft to drop bombs or torpedoes outside effective range, but neither could prevent a determined enemy, prepared to accept losses, from pressing home an attack. Similarly, gunfire was seldom effective against reconnaissance aircraft or shadowers, which could remain inside visual distance but outside gun range. The best defence against air attack was, and still is, the fighter aircraft.

The main object of defending fighters against level bombers was the disruption of the formation, in order to spoil the bomb impact distribution pattern. In this the fighters were aided by the bombers' need to fly on a steady course at a constant height and speed during their run up to the bomb release point. The return fire from a formation of bombers could be considerable, although it seldom deterred a really determined fighter attack. Once the formation was broken the individual bombers were of little offensive value and subsequent fighter victories represented bonuses, increasing the enemy's rate of attrition and reducing the morale of surviving crews.

Dive-bombers were more difficult to counter. Approaching at medium level, above 10,000 feet, they usually deployed at some distance from the target, splitting into smaller attack formations to dive on individual targets or to make a co-ordinated attack, from several directions, on a particularly attractive target – usually an aircraft carrier, if present. Even if the main formation was intercepted before deployment, dive-bombers might still get through in small numbers, and with the high degree of accuracy obtained by individual aircraft the threat to the ships was considerable. However, the diving speed of the dive-bombers was not high, being kept down to about 200 knots with the aid of air-brakes in order to maintain full control of the aircraft. As most fighters were able to dive under full control at this speed, the attack aircraft could be followed down to their release point, their concentration disturbed even if they were not shot down. The US Navy's Douglas SBD Dauntless and the Japanese Aichi D3A 'Val' dive-bombers were not easy victims, however: once their bombs had been released, they could prove to be very difficult opponents, with a respectable turn of speed and manoeuvrability which surprised more than one fighter pilot.

Fighter-bombers gradually ousted the dive-bomber as the defence of shipping improved. Considerably higher approach and attack speeds made interception more difficult, although the interceptor usually retained its speed advantage until action was joined. The accuracy of weapons delivery was not as great as that achieved by 'pure' dive-bombers, but the improved prospects of reaching the target and surviving thereafter made the fighter-bomber an attractive attack aircraft for most navies and air forces.

Torpedo attack tactics varied considerably, according to the limitations of the individual nations' weapons and aircraft. Twin-engined land-based torpedo-bombers – the German Junkers Ju 88 and Heinkel He 111, Italian Savoia Marchetti S.79, Japanese Mitsubishi G4M 'Betty', and British Bristol Beaufort and others – usually made long low-level approaches at the release speed, being limited by their size to fairly gentle manoeuvres and unable to make diving approaches due to their liability to build up speed too quickly. The US Navy's Dougles TBD Devastator also favoured the long-drawn-out low-level approach, mainly because of the torpedo limitations, but both the Royal Navy and the Japanese Navy carrier torpedo-bombers made diving attacks, one at low speed but at steep angles and the other at up to 250 knots and at shallow angles. The first, British, method posed the greater difficulty for AA gun defences, but the Japanese method was almost unstoppable once the dive had begun and before the aircraft came within AA gun range. Fighters trying to stop the Nakajima B5N 'Kate' had to be placed at the right height and be patrolling at high speed if they were to be able to reach a firing position.

As in the case of the level bombers, the land-based torpedo bombers could be forced to break away or jettison their ordnance by determined fighter attacks on approaching formations, while timely and skilful manoeuvring by the convoy or task force could also thwart attacks before torpedo release point. Once within AA gun range, the torpedo aircraft were best left alone by the fighters, for flying at low level, on a steady course at constant height, the bombers were the most vulnerable targets the ships could wish for. Not so the carrier torpedo-bombers. Only during the medium-level approach were they really vulnerable: once they had split into sub-flights of three or six aircraft, and used in conjunction with dive-bombers, the defences – gun and fighter – could easily become saturated and unable to deal with all the groups. Like the dive-bombers, they were best dealt with at long range, with the object of scattering the formation and disrupting the timing of the attack.

Shadowers and reconnaissance aircraft were priority targets if the presence of the ships was to be kept unknown to the enemy. If the aircraft could be shot down quickly enough, then there was the chance that he had been unable to make a sighting report, while the destruction of a shadower in mid-mission could result in the enemy losing touch for several hours. However, once the force was under observation by several aircraft there was little point in diverting fighters from the anti-bomber patrols.

Whenever possible, fighter escorts accompanied carrier strike aircraft. If sufficient were available, they were divided between the close escort and the top cover; the former stuck with the bombers, driving off interceptors but not becoming involved in dog-fighting, while the latter acted offensively against the interceptors, distracting them from their main task of harrying the bombers. The US Navy took this a stage further in 1944, strike days opening with a fighter sweep, by up to 120 aircraft, to clear the air for the bomber waves which followed. If no fighter defences were met before or over the target, then the close escort could be of greater assistance, attacking AA batteries and fire-control positions. Presenting less area to aim at than the strike aircraft, and with greater manoeuvrability and forward fire power, the fighters suffered relatively light losses and certainly improved the chances of survival of the main strike. The Royal Navy carried this flak-suppression task to its greatest level of efficiency in the strikes on Norwegian coastal targets during 1944: contour-hugging Grumman Wildcat and Hellcat pilots, together with cannon-armed Seafires and Fairey Fireflies, kept the heads of the flak battery gunners down so effectively that Barracuda and Avenger losses were kept below 5 per cent of attacking aircraft.

2. Aircraft and Armament

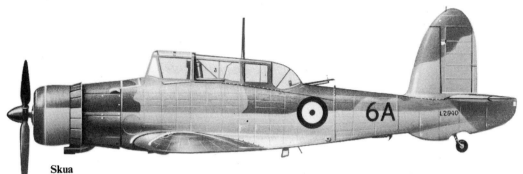

Skua
Aircraft flown by Major R. T. Partridge, R.M., and Lieutenant R. S. Bostock, CO
and Senior Observer of 800 Squadron. Ditched in Norwegian lake 27th April, 1940,
salvaged summer 1974.

At the outbreak of war, on 3rd September 1939, the Royal Navy was
armed with two fighter types, with a variant of one about to enter service.
The Blackburn Skua had entered service at the end of 1938, after a very
chequered development history, in the course of which the aircraft had
come very close to being abandoned as unusable, earlier in 1938. Designed
to a staff requirement for an aircraft which would combine the roles of
fighter and dive-bomber, the Skua was a very advanced concept for 1934,
being an all-metal monoplane with fully retractable main undercarriage –
the first naval fighter to incorporate both these marks of modernity. It was
a two-seater, carrying either an Observer to navigate on long strikes or a
Telegraphist Air-Gunner. Built to be able to withstand acceleration loads –
'g' – experienced in dive-bombing, and carrying 166 gallons of fuel, the
Skua was immensely heavy for its day – over 8,000 lb fully loaded, compared with the contemporary Hawker Hurricane's 6,500 lb. Powered by a
Bristol Perseus radial engine, delivering 905 hp at 5,000 feet, the Skua was
chronically underpowered and its maximum speed of 225 mph at 9,500 feet
was quite inadequate by 1939 standards, as was its rate of climb – fully
loaded, it took 22 minutes to reach 15,000 feet. On the credit side, the Skua
was better armed than its contemporary carrier fighters, with four wing-
mounted 0.303 in Browning machine guns and a single rear-firing free-
mounted 0.303 in Lewis gun. The pilot was provided with a reflector gun
sight for accurate aiming of the Brownings or the bombs. As a dive-bomber
the Skua could carry a 500 lb bomb nearly 300 miles to a target – the equivalent of four hours on fighter patrol over the Fleet.

As well as the dual-purpose Skua, the Royal Navy ordered a straight
fighter variant – the Roc. If the Skua was a disappointment in some
quarters, the Roc was regarded as a disaster by all! Influenced by the RAF,
which had become convinced that the turret-armed fighter was the ideal
bomber destroyer, the Admiralty ordered this turret-armed Skua, with all
armament concentrated in a four-gun power-operated turret. The fixed
weight rose by a quarter of a ton without any increase in engine power,
and the bulky turret created more drag than the single 'glasshouse' cockpit

15

Blackburn Roc interceptors of 806 Squadron. Flying with this unit from shore bases during the Dunkirk evacuation, Rocs claimed their only confirmed victory, over a Junkers Ju 88 off Belgium. (*MoD* (*N*))

Above right. Blackburn Skua in a 45° dive with dive-breaks extended. The almost vertical windscreen did little for the streamlining, but it reduced the refraction caused by the glass and was adopted to increase aiming accuracy. (*FAA Museum*)

Above centre. Gloster Sea Gladiator (N2274 was one of 22 handed over after the 1938 Munich Crisis) seen aboard USS *Wasp* in April 1942, when the American carrier began a period of loan to the British Home Fleet. (*USN 80-CF-548606-4*)

enclosure, so that the level speed was reduced to 219 mph and the 'interceptor' took three minutes longer to reach 15,000 feet. The turret-fighter idea had been based on a misconception of the capabilities of modern gun sights and of likely tactics and it turned out to be a failure in Royal Air Force service.

By 1938, when the successor to the Roc was being considered (more than a year before the production Roc appeared), it was apparent that an immediate replacement was needed for the 181 mph Hawker Nimrod biplane which was still the main Fleet fighter. Turning to the Air Force, the Navy managed to obtain a small number of Gloster Gladiator biplane interceptors on extended loan and followed this with an order for 60 Sea Gladiators, the first of which were delivered at the beginning of 1939. A relatively simple adaptation, the Sea Gladiator was only slightly slower than the Gladiator, and appreciably faster than the Skua above 8,000 feet, reaching 245 mph at 15,000 feet. The rate of climb was excellent, the fighter taking only seven minutes to reach 15,000 feet. Like the Skua, the Sea Gladiator was armed with four Brownings, aimed by a reflector sight, but two of the

Sea Gladiator
Aircraft flown by Sub Lieutenant W. E. G. Taylor of 804 Squadron from *Glorious* and *Furious* during Norwegian campaign.

guns were installed in the fuselage and their rate of fire was reduced by the need for synchronisation. No offensive load could be carried, and with a fuel tankage of only 39 gallons the endurance was too short for naval purposes, patrol length being restricted to barely an hour. High-Frequency radio-telephone (R/T) was installed (as in the Skua) with crystal-controlled push-button frequency selection, but too few ships were fitted with the necessary sets, other than the aircraft carriers.

The 1938 fighter did not appear in service until June 1940. This was a two-seat monoplane, derived from an unsuccessful light bomber design and extensively developed to suit it for the general-purpose naval fighter role. The Fairey Fulmar was therefore a large and heavy aircraft, combining the light bomber's excellent endurance with the eight-gun armament of the Spitfire and Hurricane. The Specification had been modest in its

Fulmar I
Aircraft flown by Lieutenant D. C. E. F. Gibson, Senior Pilot of 803 Squadron aboard *Formidable*, December 1940 to April 1941.

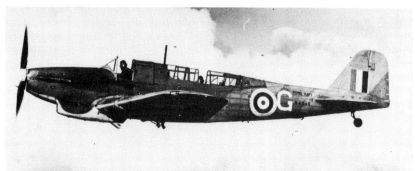

Fairey Fulmar of the RNFS Yeovilton. The vast size of the rear cockpit gave the Observer plenty of space for his navigational needs, wireless sets and, later, a radar set, but no rear gun.

(via A. Mackinnon)

demands for speed – 265 mph at 10,000 feet, but the 10,700 lb Fulmar I was badly underpowered with only 1,035 hp at 8,000 feet and it was capable of only 247 mph at that height. In service, the Fulmar's operational ceiling was little over 16,000 feet, reached in 15 minutes. The Fulmar's assets were its four-hour patrol endurance, its high diving speed (over 400 mph) and its great ammunition capacity – 750 rounds per gun in the Mark I and 1,000 rounds in the 1941 Mark II. No rear gun was provided, and the Observers and TAGs had to improvise their armament – 0.45 in Thompson sub-machine guns, 1.5 in Verey's signal pistols, and even bundles of toilet-paper held together by elastic bands, thrown out to 'burst' in the slipstream. For an aircraft of its size and weight the Fulmar was extremely manoeuvrable and its deck-landing characteristics were much liked by the pilots.

The last Royal Navy fighter Specification to be approved before the outbreak of war also called for a two-seater, with a maximum speed of 347 mph at 15,000 feet and an armament of twelve wing-mounted Brownings. This resulted in the Fairey Firefly, a four-cannon, 319 mph 'heavy fighter' which was too slow for employment in its intended role, but was, like the Fulmar, an excellent naval flying machine – as opposed to combat aircraft.

The main cause of the performance inferiority of the Royal Navy's combat aircraft was the Admiralty's acceptance of the Air Ministry's ill-founded assertion that the Fleet would not have to face land-based aircraft other than long-range patrol aircraft. If the Fleet did come within range of other shore-based aircraft, then RAF protection would be provided. Given these assurances, the Skua and Fulmar were all that were needed offensively and defensively as they need never encounter land-based fighters or modern high-speed bombers.

Fortunately for the United States and Imperial Japanese Navies, there was no third Service to insist on a false doctrine of the 'Indivisibility of Air Power'. The naval air forces were therefore allowed to develop along the lines which experience, not expediency, dictated. Both began with short-range interceptors, for purely defensive tasks, but by the end of the '30s had progressed to develop long-range fighters intended to match any opposition which might be encountered.

In 1939, the Japanese Navy had a technical edge over the US Navy. In 1937, the Mitsubishi A5M (the fifth carrier fighter – A – design for the Navy, designed by Mitsubishi – M), had entered service. A fixed-undercarriage low-wing monoplane with an open cockpit, the A5M (later to be code-named 'Claude' by the US forces) was the Japanese fighter pilot's idea of what an aeroplane should be – light (under 4,000 lb fully loaded) and therefore highly manoeuvrable and fast-climbing (less than four minutes to 10,000 feet). With only 610 hp available from its British-designed engine, the A5M2 was capable of over 260 mph at 10,000 feet, making it by far the fastest fighter of its day. Armament consisted of two synchronised Type 89 7.7 mm machine guns, aimed by means of a telescopic sight. Two 66 lb bombs could be carried, or a single 35 gallon jettisonable fuel tank, with which the fighter's endurance was over three hours.

The US Navy's standard fighter in 1939 was the Grumman biplane F3F (third naval fighter – first F – built by Grumman – second F). The

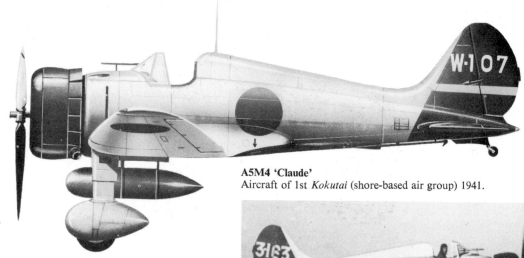

A5M4 'Claude'
Aircraft of 1st *Kokutai* (shore-based air group) 1941.

Mitsubishi Type 96
Carrier Fighter – the
A5M2 'Claude' –
seen in flight over its
first theatre of
operations, the
Hankow area of
China. (*Shuppan-
Kyodo Co.*)

Grumman F3F-3
Aircraft of VF-5, aboard *Yorktown*, 1940.

F3F-2 entered service in 1938, powered by a 950 hp Wright Cyclone R-1820-22 with a two-stage supercharger, giving the fighter a maximum speed of 256 mph at 15,000 feet – a height which was reached in a little more than six minutes. In 1939, the aerodynamically-refined F3F-3 joined the Fleet, retaining the same engine, but with a maximum speed of 263 mph.

The F3F family brought the biplane configuration to its limit. Highly manoeuvrable (although it could not be spun safely), with an excellent rate of climb and patrol endurance, the F3F-3 also introduced the heavy (0.50 in) machine gun as a permanent feature in US Navy fighters. Earlier American fighters had had 'provision' for the 0.50 in in place of one of the two 0.30 in Browning guns, but this had seldom been mounted in embarked

Opposite Right.
The first unit to
equip with the
Grumman F4F was
804 Squadron;
aircrew can be seen
examining one of the
ex-French G-36As
received in September
1940. The 0.50 in
Colt machine guns
are further apart
than the US Navy's
F4F-3 installation.

aircraft. Unfortunately, this increase in fire power was not matched by an improvement in fire control, for the F3F retained the telescopic gun sight. Although faster than the British carrier fighters, the Grumman had very little performance advantage over the standard Japanese land-based medium bomber – the Mitsubishi G3M2 'Nell' and was some 10 mph slower than the later models of the A5M carrier fighter. Nevertheless, the F3F-3 continued to serve until 1941, when the Grumman F4F-3 monoplane entered US Navy service.

The first monoplane had been the Brewster F2A-1 – the winner of a 1938 competition in which the Grumman F4F-2 had been the only other serious contender. The XF2A had been slightly slower than the XF4F, but its handling qualities were superior, so that it had received the production order while the XF4F was returned to Grumman for further development.

Apart from being the first US Navy monoplane fighter, the F2A-1's main claim to fame was that it was the first shipboard fighter to be credited with a speed in level flight of over 300 mph – 301 mph at 17,000 feet. Armament consisted of one 0.30 in and one 0.50 in machine guns firing through the airscrew arc, with a telescopic gun sight. No pilot armour or fuel tank protection was provided, so that the 5,055 lb aircraft was very manoeuvrable and had a high rate of climb – 3,000 feet per minute being claimed.

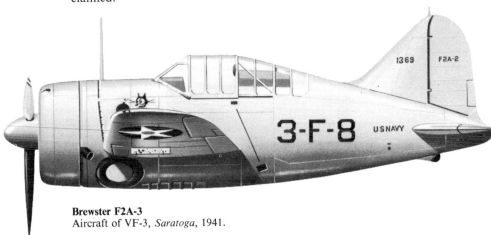

Brewster F2A-3
Aircraft of VF-3, *Saratoga*, 1941.

Brewster B-339
'Buffalo' – the
export version of the
F2A-2 – seen at RN
Air Station Hatston
after it had been
handed over for
service evaluation by
804 Squadron in
July 1940.

Only 10 F2A-1s actually served with the US Navy, from late 1939, the remainder being diverted to Finland via Sweden in the opening months of 1940. The next model – the F2A-2, began to enter service in September 1940, after Brewster had completed production of a series of similar aircraft for the Belgian Government. With a 1,200 hp Cyclone in place of the -1's 940 hp engine, the new model was appreciably faster, 323 mph being claimed at 16,000 feet, but the heavier (more realistic) armament of four 0.50 in guns added to the weight and the rate of climb fell to 2,500 feet per minute, while manoeuvrability also suffered. The Royal Navy obtained a number of the Belgian B-339s in the summer of 1940 and were most unimpressed: fitted with armour, performance and manoeuvrability were seriously degraded, and a typical example could attain only 270 mph at 6,000 feet. In October 1940, the Royal Navy's Mediterranean Fleet was struggling to keep a single Fulmar squadron up to strength, but after trying the 'Buffalo', the pilots announced that they would rather use Sea Gladiator biplanes!

Fortunately for both the Royal and United States Navies, the Grumman monoplane was completely successful in its developed form. The XF4F-3 first flew in early 1939 and a production order was placed in August. Performance and handling were better than the F2A's and orders were also placed by the French and Greek Governments. The French Navy contract was given priority after the outbreak of war in Europe, and these aircraft were 'inherited' by Britain after the fall of France in June 1940. The first squadron – 804 Squadron – was equipped with Grumman 'Martlets' in

Variations on an airframe: (Above right. the six-gun folding-wing Martlet II entered service with the Royal Navy late in 1941, but the equivalent F4F-4 Wildcat (left.) did not become operational until the late spring of 1942. Differences between the 881 Squadron Martlet being flagged off HMS *Illustrious* and the VF-6 Wildcat rolling down *Enterprise's* deck include the lack of a supercharger air intake lip in the engine cowling and the provision of external catapult pick-up points behind the blanked-off bottom windows on the British version (*IWM A15112A and USN 80-G-14116*)

September 1940, three months before the US Navy allocated its first F4F-3s to a front-line unit.

The ex-French aircraft had been built with pilot and fuel tank protection, and a reflector sight was fitted from the outset, but these refinements were not incorporated in US Navy aircraft until 1941 – gunsight – and early 1942 – protection. Although heavier than the F2A-2, it was more manoeuvrable and its rate of climb was higher, although it took over seven minutes to reach 15,000 feet. The Royal Navy again found that the performance was lower than that claimed, but the ability to reach 305 mph at 15,000 feet and about 285 mph at sea level meant that its Martlet was the fastest fighter available for embarked operations until mid-1941.

The main disadvantage of the F4F-3, named 'Wildcat' by the US Navy in 1942 (but not until 1944 by the British), was its lack of wing-folding arrangements. In the autumn of 1940, a folding-wing variant was ordered, incorporating British R/T, modified undercarriage, and two more 0.50 in guns. The US Navy also ordered the folding-wing fighter, which entered British service in late 1941 but was not in American squadron service until the late spring of 1942.

The Imperial Japanese Navy began to review its Fleet fighter requirements as soon as the war in China began, in 1937. By the following October, a specification had been issued for a fighter which would have a maximum level speed of 311 mph at 13,000 feet, a sustained rate of climb of 2,800 feet per minute up to 10,000 feet, a maximum endurance (with external fuel if necessary) of between six and eight hours, and an armament of two 20 mm cannon and two 7.7 mm machine guns. The aircraft was to weigh no more than five and a half pounds per engine horse-power: as the powerplants available in Japan in the late '30s were in the 1,000 hp range, this effectively limited the maximum all-up weight to 5,500 lb – less than the empty weight of a Grumman F4F-3.

Incredibly, Mitsubishi met the specification and in some respects exceeded it. A service trials unit saw combat in pre-production A6M2 Type O Carrier Fighters in China from August 1940. No major problems arose during design or development, or during the service trials period, and quantity production was ordered on 31st July 1940. By the end of the year several carrier-based *Sentai* had been re-armed with the A6M, and on the outbreak of war in the Pacific all but a few front-line units had handed over their A5Ms in favour of the 'Zero-Sen'.

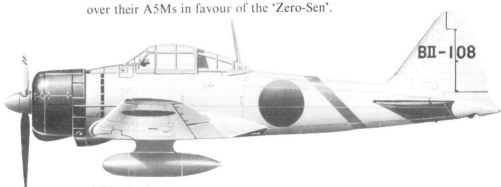

A6M2 'Zero'
Aircraft of 2nd *Koku Sentai* (*Hiryu* and *Soryu*) – assigned to *Hiryu* 1941–42.

With maximum speeds of 280 mph at sea level and 325 mph at 16,000 feet, the A6M2 Model 21 could climb to 15,000 feet in five minutes – faster than either the Spitfire or the Bf109E. Its manoeuvrability was to become legendary – at speeds of less than 200 knots no other monoplane fighter could remain in a turn with it, although many tried. In the hands of the well-trained aggressive pilots of 1941, the 'Zero' demonstrated that it was the Japanese Navy which had best absorbed the lessons of the preceding 20 years. In one airframe, Mitsubishi had combined all the attributes of the ideal naval fighter, capable of defending the Fleet, escorting strikes, and achieving local air superiority over land-based fighter opposition. The A6M had one inferiority: its light weight was achieved by omitting all protection and by using a lightly constructed, highly-stressed structure – if hit it either caught fire or crumpled up. It was therefore a fighter which should always have held the initiative and dictated the terms of a combat: while the first generation of Japanese pilots were the most experienced pilots in the Far East, these conditions held good.

The best all-round naval fighter of the early years of the war was undoubtedly the Mitsubishi Type 0 – the deadly A6M2 'Zero-Sen'.

Armament

The Royal Navy began the war with the 0.303 in Browning machine gun, which weighed less than 25 lb and had a rate of fire of some 1,200 rounds per minute. The maximum range was only about 300–400 yards and as bomber protection improved, so the fighter had to close in to point-blank to achieve the number of hits and penetration needed to inflict serious damage. By 1941, the 0.303 in was of little use against European aircraft targets, although the use of incendiary explosive 'De Wilde' projectiles allowed the fighters to continue scoring victories until a heavier weapon arrived.

This was the 20 mm cannon, designed by either the Hispano or Oerlikon firms. The Hispano Mk II 20 mm cannon fired an explosive shell, at the rate of between 600 and 700 rounds per minute at a high muzzle velocity (2,750 feet per second). The gun weighed four times as much as the 0.303 in Browning, but its halved rate of fire was more than outweighed by the effect of hits by the heavy explosive shells from just two or four guns, few strikes being needed to inflict fatal damage. The Oerlikon was slower-firing – less than 600 rounds per minute – and its muzzle velocity was

Left.
In May 1944, the US Navy began experiments with a 4-cannon Corsair, the F4U-1C. Only one carrier operated this model of Corsair, *Intrepid's* VF-10 and VBF-10 taking it into action off Okinawa in March 1945. (*USN*)

Right.
Late production models of the 'Zero' were armed with the long-barrelled faster-firing Mark II version of the Type 99 (Oerlikon) 20 mm cannon, and, outboard, a copy of the 0.5 in Browning – the 13.2 mm Type 3 machine gun. The Allied code-name for the type was 'Zeke 52c'.

1

2

3

4

Aircraft Guns

1) the 0.303 in Browning used by most British fighters. High rate of fire but lacked penetration against post-1940 aircraft.

2) the 0.50 in Browning standard in American fighters. Japanese copy had higher rate of fire (850 rpm v 800 rpm) but lower muzzle velocity).

3) 20 mm Type 99-I cannon – Oerlikon design manufactured under licence in Japan. Lighter than 0.50 in, but fired heavier shell at lower rpm.

4) 20 mm Hispano Mk II cannon – licence built by British and Americans. Weighed 99 lb – 35 lb more than 0.50 in – but had high m/v and projectile which weighed twice as much as the 0.50 in.

809 Squadron personnel examine a belt of 0.303 in incendiary ammunition as it is fed into the tanks of a Fulmar in HMS *Victorious*'s hangar. (*IWM A7649*)

Royal Navy armourers belting 20 mm Hispano cannon ammunition for 807 Squadron Seafires at an airfield in Ceylon. Note the considerably greater size of the 20 mm round, compared with the 0.303 in round. (*FAA Museum*)

initially less than 2,000 feet per second, and its projectile was lighter than the Hispano's. Fitted in the early cannon-armed Hurricane and Sea Hurricane, its main application to a naval fighter was in the Japanese A6M. Built under licence as the 'Type 99 Aircraft Machine Gun', the light weight of the gun made it suitable for the light Japanese fighter. During the War, a Model II Type 99 appeared, with a slightly higher rate of fire and a greater muzzle velocity, but even after modification it was still inferior to the Hispano, which was fitted to late-production models of the Grumman Hellcat and the Vought Corsair, as well as the British Sea Hurricane, Seafire, and Firefly.

The favoured American air weapon was the 0.50 in Browning machine gun – possibly the best fighter weapon of the war. Weighing only 64 lb, the 0.50 in fired a solid shot or incendiary projectile at a slightly higher

Opposite.

Above,
rectangular rear
view mirror and
small GM II
reflector sight of
Lieutenant A. B.
Fraser-Harris's 807
Squadron Seafire
IIC (*FAA Museum*)

Centre,
small simian adjusts
the circular rear
view mirror of an
888 Squadron
Martlet II; sight is a
US Navy/Army
N-2N (*D. R.
Whittaker*)

Below,
'shaving mirror' on
extension arm was
standard on Seafire
LIII, but the GGS
IID gyro-gunsight
(seen in raised
position) was a later
modification. Pilot
is Lieutenant G.
Stevens, a New
Zealander serving
with 880 Squadron.
(*M. Crosley*)

muzzle velocity than the 20 mm Hispano, at a rate of between 850 and 950 rounds per minute. Penetration characteristics were superior to those of the 20 mm over a longer range, but the non-explosive rounds lacked the splinter effect of the cannon shells for ground attack. From 1944, the Japanese began to produce a copy of the big Browning, the 'Type 3 "13 mm" Aircraft Machine Gun'. Even lighter than the original, it featured some improvements, but it was not widely used in fighters, apart from installation in some late production models of the A6M.

The principal Japanese light machine gun was the 'Type 89', installed in the A5M 'Claude' and A6M as a synchronised weapon, mounted above the engine. Of nominal 7.7. mm calibre, it was in fact a copy of the British World War One Vickers gun, chambered to take rimmed 0.303 in rounds. The maximum rate of fire was only 750 rounds per minute.

The positioning of the armament in the wings of most fighters designed after 1936, as opposed to the fuselage installations enjoyed from 1916 to 1936, brought the need for accurate alignment of guns with the sight. In most cases, the wing guns were 'toed-in' to converge at a point ahead of the aircraft, within the range of the guns – 250 yards in the case of the 0.303 in Browning, for example. In late 1940, not entirely satisfied with the results of convergent alignment, the Royal Navy devised a pattern intended to fill a volume of air with as many bullets as possible, as opposed to trying to hit a single point with all the bullets. The results were remarkable. In 1941, Fulmars fitted with the two harmonisation systems destroyed similar numbers of enemy aircraft (35), but only three fighters with the 'Admiralty Standard Harmonisation' were shot down by return fire, in contrast with eleven whose guns were aligned to a point, and which had apparently had to close to short range to score their kills.

The Royal Navy started the war with the reflector gun sight as standard in its fighters. The sight consisted of a small 'black' box' mounted behind the windscreen; above the box was mounted an inclined optically-flat glass screen, on which a simple sighting 'picture' was projected. The pilot saw a central aiming dot, which represented the line-of-flight axis of the aircraft and its fixed guns; around the dot was a circle which represented a 50-knot target crossing speed at a given range, and radial lines extending outwards from the dot. To reach a hitting position, the fighter pilot aligned his aircraft so that the target was flying towards the central dot, using the radial lines as reference marks, and so that the enemy reached the appropriate crossing speed circle at the desired range. The relative crossing speed had to be estimated by the pilot, as did the range, but properly used the sight would give the correct deflection or 'lead' to enable the pilot to aim far enough ahead of the target to score hits. The real advantage of this simple sight was its easy interpretation under all combat conditions and its non-distracting presentation: focused at infinity it allowed the pilot to concentrate on the target without having to readjust his eyes to fixed 'iron sights' less than two feet in front of him and align the bead backsight with the deflection rings on the foresight and the target. The telescope sights fitted to American and Japanese fighters until 1941 had the disadvantage of reducing the pilot's field of vision in combat – a most undesirable feature in a crowded sky.

Even before the other navies began to install reflector sights, Britain had

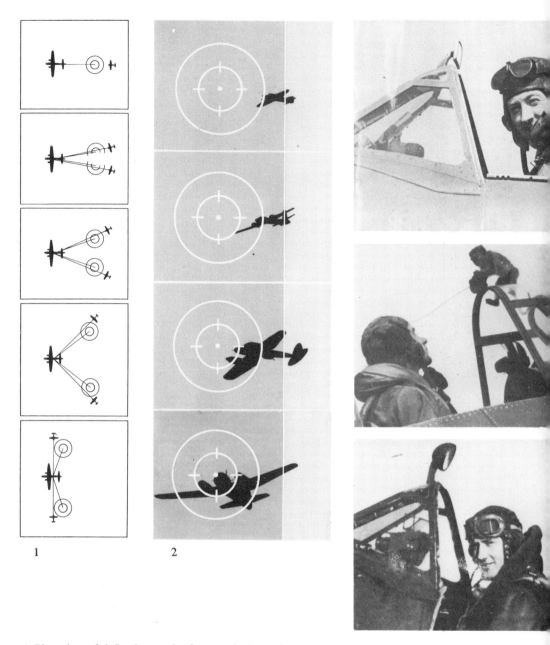

1 Plan view of deflection angles for a typical attack.

2 View through a Reflector Sight: the deflection or 'lead' is assessed by the pilot
as a relative crossing speed and the fighter is flown to place the target on the
appropriate radius ('rad'), flying towards the centre of the sight picture. As
the fighter closes the range and drops astern of the target, so the deflection
needed decreases. Many sights did not have the second (in this case 100-knot)
deflection ring.

The gyro-gunsight picture: the six 'diamonds' were set around the wing-tips of the target and the central 'pipper' on the cockpit – by tracking the target's path through space and increasing the diameter of the ring of diamonds, the 'rate precession gyros' fed the deflection needed to the sight, moving the picture away from the centre.

begun work on a lead-computing gun sight. Intended originally for turret guns, the new sight used gyroscopes to measure the rate of angular change and range rate of change of a target to provide a firing solution. Six radial 'diamonds' indicated the wingspan of the target, a figure which was set on the sight controls by the pilot, and by clipping the outline of the target with the diamonds (the diameter being controlled by a throttle twist-grip) as the range decreased, a range change rate was fed into the sight. Angular change of rate was provided by the pilot using a 'pipper' in the centre of the ring of diamonds to track the target's path relative to the fighter; pitch, roll and yaw gyros in the sight precessed as the pilot kept the pipper on the target, and the rate of precession was measured and used to generate a movement of the picture away from the actual centre-line of the sight, thus giving the deflection. The initial disadvantage of the gyro gun sight, introduced into RAF service in 1942 and Royal Navy service in early 1944, was that a period of ranging and tracking was needed to enable the sight to compute the deflection angle: while this was available when attacking a bomber on a steady course, it was not always available in a dog-fight, when to fly on a predictable path for any length of time was to court disaster. A 'fixed cross' aiming point could be displayed to cater for these conditions, but this lacked the crossing rate references and deflection corrections had to be made by 'guesstimation'. The GGS was also readily adaptable to the needs of bomb and rocket aiming, with variations of the pipper and diamond picture or the cross being used for compensating for such ballistic phenomena as 'trail' and 'gravity drop', as well as for wind

An 804 Squadron
Sea Gladiator breaks
away after a dummy
$\frac{1}{4}$-attack on a
Swordfish over
Scapa Flow. The
'target' has been
banking towards the
direction of the
attack to make the
fighter pull harder
and increase his
deflection problem.
(*MoD* (*N*))

speed and direction. Built in America as the Mark 18 and 23 Gunsights, the British GGS Mark II was one of the more important examples of reverse Lend-Lease.

Even after the most careful attention had been paid to the design of the gun sight and the alignment of the guns with the sight, hits were not guaranteed. The deflection indicated to the pilot was calculated on the time of flight of the projectile as well as on the speed of the target: at high altitudes the resistance of the air was much less than at sea level, so that the projectile velocity was sustained for longer and the effective range was almost doubled. A compromise was made between the two conditions, so that the sight would give the exact deflection under only one combination of temperature and pressure, but with only slight discrepancies at the upper and lower extremes.

Another source of inaccuracy lay in the possible lack of rigidity in the airframe. The guns were aligned with the aircraft jacked up in the flying position – a position which was very accurately determined by means of plumb lines and spirit levels on the individual guns – but with the engine stopped. The rotation of the propeller in flight imposed torsional (twisting) stress on the wings, which, combined with the considerable vibration and the aerodynamic effects of manoeuvring flight, could mean that the guns would no longer be aligned with the sight. A discrepancy of half a degree at a firing range of 300 yards meant a difference of seven feet (greater than the depth of a fighter fuselage) between aiming and impact points. The ruggedly built US Navy fighters were less prone to wing flexing than the British and Japanese aircraft, a virtue which, with the effectiveness of the 0.50 in gun, gave the American and British pilots who flew Grumman and Vought fighters a considerable advantage in combat.

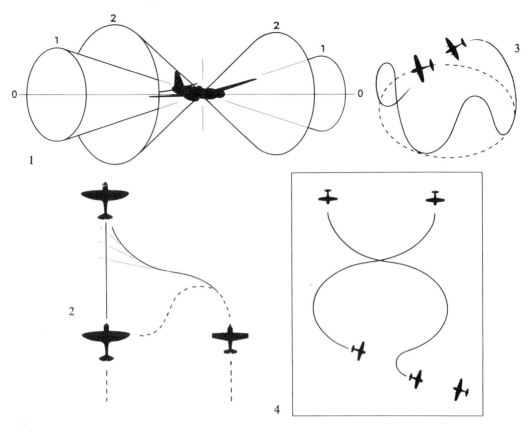

1 Bomber gunners also had deflection problems, and this drawing, adapted from an American training sketch, illustrates the deflection 'cones' around a 200-knot 'Betty' bomber.

2 The Quarter Attack, also known as the High Side or Beam Attack. Bearing and elevation would be changing rapidly.
The pass was intended to begin with the fighter on 'the perch', about 400 yards on the beam and 500 feet above the target; the fighter then turned in towards the target and dived, reversing the turn before the target crossed the fighter's line of flight. The fighter thus presented a head-on target until the target was within range of its guns; thereafter the bomber's gunners were provided with problems of azimuth and vertical deflection, while the fighter pilot's deflection reduced at a constant rate.

3 The 'Yo-yo' or 'climb and dive' manoeuvre, used to reduce the radius of turn by a fighter engaging a slower but tighter-turning opponent: by pulling up into a series of near-stall turns, the faster fighter could reduce speed and thus wing-over steeply, so that in the subsequent dive its flight-path cut across that of the enemy, thus permitting the pilot to gain a firing position at intervals.

4 The 'Thach Weave', or 'Scissors': intended to improve the look-out field of view of fighters and to enable aircraft scissoring together to come to one another's assistance immediately. Introduced to the US Navy by Lieutenant Commander J. S. Thach in order to minimise the F4F-3's inferiority to the 'Zero', it became the standard defensive and offensive manoeuvre in enemy airspace.

3. Training

Although the training of a fighter pilot followed the same lines in the various navies, there were nevertheless considerable differences between the systems and, therefore, the products. Under the pressure of war, the training of pilots had to be on mass-production lines and changes were inevitable if an increasing flow was to be maintained. The effects of these changes were completely different within the three major navies.

The Imperial Japanese Navy pilots of the five carrier-borne Air Flotillas (*Koku Sentai*) operational in December 1941 were among the most highly-trained and experienced fighter pilots of their day. Up to 1939, about 100 pilots had been trained every year for all Japanese Naval Air Force tasks – ship- and shore-based. The original flying training syllabi had been drawn up by British former naval air officers, and as modified by the Japanese they were methodical and extremely thorough.

The selection procedures were rigorous and wastage during training was high – 33 to 40 per cent – reflecting the high standard of training required. The majority of the pilots were enlisted men – Naval Air Pilots – selected from applicants aged between 14 and 20 years of age who had completed at least two years of secondary education. The younger trainees were given a 30-month educational course before flying training commenced. During the eight-month flying training course, the pilots flew just over 100 hours and were given an extremely thorough ground-school education: after the war, US Navy officers wryly admitted that the average Japanese Naval Air Pilot had a wider knowledge of the theory of flight and engine design than junior officer pilots in the US Navy.

Relatively few officers were trained before the war. All but a few reservists were selected from Naval Academy graduates with two years of sea duty and therefore needed no general education before commencing 'pre-flight' course – a two-month general lead-in to explain the basics of aircraft design, flying controls, engine theory, meteorology, navigation, and so forth. Thereafter, the officer aircrew passed through a ten-month flying course, at the end of which they had flown between 150 and 175 hours. As leaders they were expected to have a higher standard of training and knowledge than the NAPs, and tactical leadership training was part of the extended syllabus.

The flying training for NAPs and officers was divided into equal portions – basic training and advanced/operational training. On leaving the operational fighter training school at Oita, the new pilot was sent to join an Air Group (*Kokutai*) belonging to one of the land-based Air Flotillas. The 'depot' Air Groups such as the Sasebo, Yokohama or Ominato units served as 'pools' for the front-line units, providing additional training for the pilots in preparation for their first assignment to an operational Air Flotilla, usually shore-based. Not until the pilot had gained considerable experience and then shown himself to be 'above average' would he be considered for one of the carrier Air Flotillas. Thus, before 1942 over five years might elapse between the pilot leaving fighter school and joining his carrier unit. The war with China had been in progress for more than four years when the Pacific War began, so that with the system of rotation used by the JNAF all the carrier pilots, manning 108 A6M2 'Zeroes' and 49 A5M4 'Claudes', had gained combat experience, as had most of the pilots assigned to the three land-based fighter Air Groups which were armed with 220 A6M2s.

Although combat losses during the first six months of the Pacific War were not heavy, the Japanese had to draw upon the shore-based Air Groups to maintain their carrier fighter pilot strength. As early as March 1942, over half the pilots in the *Tainan Kokutai* were sent back to Japan from the East Indies to undergo carrier training. The losses during the second half of 1942 were very heavy indeed, the land-based units suffering as heavily in the bitter fighting in the Solomons and over New Guinea as the carriers did in the four great naval battles (Coral Sea, Midway, Eastern Solomons and Santa Cruz) which cost the Navy six carriers and over 500 aircraft of all types.

Replacement of lost pilots from the existing 'pipe-line' system was inadequate. The general education of enlisted candidates could not be reduced to cut the length of training, and the ground-school syllabus also remained at its pre-war length. Apart from a rather larger NAP candidate intake, the only major alteration in recruiting policy was the training of reserve officer aircrew. These men had to be college graduates, aged less than 28, with the necessary physical qualifications – 5 feet height, 105 lb (7 stones 7 lb) weight, 31 inches girth of chest. By 1944, there were 4,700 reserve officer pilots, compared with only 650 regular officers and approximately 7,000 enlisted pilots. The JNAF was, however, always limited by the relatively small number of potential pilots available in an under-educated and under-nourished country.

The full effects of the 1942 carrier pilot losses were not felt immediately, for there were still sufficient pilots to man the surviving carrier Air Flotillas, and the training system supplied enough new men to enable the JNAF to expand the units intended for new and repaired carriers. In April 1943, the carrier units, which had not seen action since the previous November, were 'loaned' to Rabaul, where the land-based 11th Air Fleet (*Kantai*) had been taking heavy losses. The carrier aircraft achieved little and suffered severe casualties. From this stage, the situation grew even worse: 97 fighters had been lost in action during the first three months of 1943, 178 were lost between April and June, and 335 between July and September – pilot losses were about half of the total. In the autumn of 1943, the JNAF decided to dispense with the advanced and operational training phase of training, having previously reduced intermediate training by 10 flying hours to 45 hours for NAPs and 65 hours for officers. Pilots now went direct to combat units, where they received brief conversion training and

tactical instruction before going into action with about 100 hours flight time. Although this meant an immediate increase in the number of pilots available to the Air Flotillas, the inexperienced pilots enjoyed brief lives – 385 JNAF fighters were lost in combat during the last quarter of 1943. The lack of properly qualified instructors to supervise conversion training from the 340 hp, 132 mph K5Y 'Willow' biplane intermediate trainer to the 1,100 hp, 335 mph A6M3 'Hamp' retracting-undercarriage monoplane resulted in very high attrition during conversion. During the last quarter of 1943, 469 fighters were lost from non-combat causes, compared with only 213 in the first quarter. These losses, incurred in the main as a result of training accidents, rose to 524 in the first three months of 1944. Alarmed by this increasing drain on a force already bled white in combat, the Naval Staff ordered a return to the pre-1943 system.

By 1944, the situation had deteriorated to such an extent that even this improvement in pilot training could do little to help the JNAF. Combat losses increased as the American advance in the Pacific continued, and after the invasion of the Philippines in October 1944 the supply of aviation fuel from the East Indies was drastically reduced. Fuel allocations to training units were cut almost immediately and further reductions followed, until by July 1945 only sufficient for 15 flying hours per trainee per month was allowed.

The contrast between the Imperial Japanese and United States Navies was extreme. Although well trained, the American carrier pilots had no combat experience at the outbreak of war, other than that gleaned from the Royal Navy, which was fighting a very different kind of war. With a large population, with a high standard of education, the US Navy had little difficulty in recruiting personnel of the required calibre and, backed by the country's vast industrial resources, the rapidly-expanded training organisation was capable of producing pilots in ever-increasing numbers.

Like the JNAF, the US Navy's aviation forces were an *élite*, carefully selected from many volunteers, thoroughly trained, and led by aviators (Captains of carriers had to be qualified pilots – a policy which resulted in the emergence of some grey-feathered fledglings, the most notable of whom was W. F. Halsey, awarded 'Wings' in 1934, at the age of 52!).

In 1943, the Japanese Navy began to send their trainee fighter pilots direct to front-line units for operational training. Here a pilot instructor of one of the shore-based air groups supervises the starting of an A6M5c 'Zeke' 's engine.

The standard intermediate trainer for most Allied naval fighter pilots from 1941 was the North American SNJ (as used by the US Navy) or Harvard (in British service). Harvard IIs of No 31 Service Flying Training School, Kingston, Ontario, were used exclusively for training Royal Navy pilots to 'Wings' standard. (*P. J. Spelling*)

Unlike the JNAF, the US Navy had no operational shore-based fighter squadrons, so that on completion of the fighter school course the new pilot was sent to a carrier squadron. Enlisted men, entered on a special scheme – the 'V-5' – or taken from volunteers from serving enlisted men, made up nearly half of a squadron's pilot complement, these 'Aviation Pilots' or 'Aviation Machinists' all having Petty Officer or Chief Petty Officer status. Officer aircrew were either selected from serving 'Line Officers' or entered as Aviation Cadets – 'AvCads'. The length of flying training and the syllabus were identical for officers and enlisted men.

In June and July 1940, President Roosevelt approved a vast expansion in the size of the Navy, including the aviation element, which was to be allowed to increase to a maximum of 15,000 aircraft. The intensive recruiting programme which followed took sufficient time to permit the Navy to expand its training facilities to cope with the numbers.

In June 1940, the Navy's only flying training centre, Pensacola, was accepting approximately fifty student pilots per month, to fill all Navy and Marine Corps requirements. Within a year, two other centres, at Jacksonville, Florida, and Corpus Christi, Texas, had been opened and the three centres were taking a combined total of 190 students per month. Of the total of 3,000 trainees in the pipe-line, about 900 were intended for carrier squadrons, 300 for fighters.

On 7th December 1941, the US Navy had nine front-line fighter squadrons, each with 18 aircraft, with about 200 embarked or assigned pilots. By recalling Reserve pilots, the US Navy had 6,000 trained pilots and 5,000 under training a month after Pearl Harbour, when Roosevelt approved a further increase in the naval air forces – to 27,500 aircraft. To man this vast number of aircraft, the Navy was faced with qualifying 30,000 pilots per year – 700 had been trained during 1940 and more than double that number in 1941. Instead of 200 trainees joining the centres each month, there would have to be 2,500!

US Navy initial deck-landing training took place aboard either USS *Wolverine* (illustrated) or USS *Sable*, a pair of large paddle-wheelers fitted with 500-feet flight decks during 1942. Wildcats from NAS Glenview provided the mounts for this training, carried out in the U-boat-free waters of Lake Michigan. (*US Navy*)

By dint of ingenuity and hard work, but without taking any short cuts, the requirement was exceeded within 18 months of the demand. By July 1943, 44,979 pilots were in the pipe-line which stretched 64 weeks between commencing Flight Preparatory Training and joining a squadron; statistics indicated that 41,319 would be awarded their 'Navy Wings of Gold'. This staggering number of pilots by no means exhausted the source of supply, for in July 1943, there were another 23,000 accepted candidates awaiting Preparatory training – an eight-month queue which did not shorten until a year later, when recruiting was cut back.

Elementary training was handled by 92 civilian flying schools throughout the United States, these being under contract to the Civil Aviation Authority War Training Service. After three months of basic flying instruction on light aircraft, the AvCad was sent to a Pre-Flight School for three months of 'navalisation training' on the parade ground, in the gymnasium, and in the lecture room, before going on to one of sixteen Primary Training Schools, where he would learn to fly competently. Assuming that he was one of the seventeen out of twenty to pass this stage, the student then went on to either Pensacola or Corpus Christi for Intermediate Flight Training, being streamed towards a specialisation at last. At this stage the streaming consisted of allocation to 'Carrier, 'Patrol Bomber', or 'Observation' training schedules.

To refer to 'Pensacola or Corpus Christi' without explanation is misleading. They were literally centres, each with six auxiliary air stations, which in turn had numerous satellite fields – forty-seven were retained *after* the war, the other ninety or so being closed down. After about four months in these 'pilot factories' the AvCads who passed the course were awarded their Wings and commissioned as Ensigns. The 'Carrier' pilots then went on to Miami, where they were at last allocated to a role and spent a month learning to fly carrier-type aircraft.

During 'Intermediate' the emphasis had been on learning how to use

Opposite.

After formation of the Air Group, the squadrons embarked for their carrier's 'shake-down' cruise when possible. During the July 1943 work-up aboard USS *Bunker Hill*, it was decided that the Corsairs of VF-17 were not suitable for shipboard operations and the type was therefore not used extensively by the US Navy until 1945. (*USN 80-G-204784*)

the aircraft, as well as fly it under more demanding conditions. Operational Training was centred on Jacksonville, which administered three (later six) fighter out-stations, where the student pilots carried out intensive weaponry training and practised the tactical drills and skills which they would need in combat units. After two months at 'Jax', the new fighter pilot was sent to Glenview, Illinois, for deck-landing training aboard one of the two training carriers (*Wolverine* and *Sable*) based on Lake Michigan. During the winter, when the lake was frozen, pilots intended for the Pacific Fleet carried out their 'carrier qualification' practices aboard a carrier off the California coast, while Atlantic Fleet fighter pilots were sent to Norfolk, Virginia. After 'Carquals' the pilot was considered qualified and was appointed to a fighter squadron. With between 360 and 450 hours in his log-book, he was by far the most extensively and thoroughly trained 'new boy' of his day.

The real strength of the training system lay in its instructors. Pilots from the Fleet were fed back in as instructors from 'Basic' onwards, and they were able to pass on their confidence and experience to the students during the vital early stages of flying training. Certain outstanding Ensigns were trained as instructors as soon as they had completed 'Intermediate', simply to provide the number of instructors required, but Operational Training was given only by pilots who had seen front-line service.

On joining his first front-line squadron, ashore at an Air Station, the fighter pilot would discover that training was by no means finished. His Squadron Commanding Officer, the Division leaders, and perhaps one or two Section leaders would be veterans of at least one combat 'tour', but fully 75 per cent would be like himself, in need of the thorough drilling to be given by the men who would lead them into action and whose tails they would have to guard. Fighter tactics, gunnery practices, ground attack, navigation formation, and carrier circuit drills, all would have to be flown again and again, until the CO was entirely satisfied that every pilot knew all the calls and all the plays. Then the squadron would practise with the dive-bomber and torpedo-bomber squadrons in the same Air Group and which would embark in the same carrier.

After a work-up which might last up to six months, the Air Group would join a carrier, taking its own aircraft to a ship in American waters, or inheriting those of an Air Group being relieved aboard a carrier in a forward area. In the first case, the squadrons would benefit from the ship's 'shake-down' period and passage to the operational area to gain experience of carrier flying: many ships took a swipe at one of the by-passed Japanese islands – Wake, Mili or Wotje – to give the Air Group a taste of combat. Joining a fully-operational ship during one of its short breaks from operations, the Air Group might have only a day or so to settle down before engaging the enemy. During the four-to-six-month tour of duty aboard the carrier, losses would be made up from the 'pool' of reserve aircraft and trained pilots maintained in the forward area. Losses were in fact relatively light, thanks to the high regard for the value of aircrew life held by the operational commanders: by using aircraft, submarines and surface ships as 'lifeguards', often placed in positions of great risk, the US Navy retrieved hundreds of downed aircrew who would otherwise have been lost.

US Marine Corps pilots took fighters to sea in January 1945, to reinforce

the carriers which were under heavy pressure due to the success of the Japanese suicide tactics. Eight USMC Corsair squadrons served aboard *Essex*-class carriers during 1945, and four escort carrier Air Groups were entirely Marine-manned by 15th August – VJ-Day.

At the end of the war, the US Navy and Marine Corps had over 6,000 fighter pilots with front-line squadrons – more than there had been for all flying duties in December 1941. And it is worth remembering that the US Navy was America's second biggest air force!

By contrast with the United States and Imperial Japanese Navies, the Royal Navy was a very poor relation. Not until May 1939 had it finally broken away from the Royal Air Force, upon which it had been dependent since 1918 for the provision of aircraft and aircrew training. A steady flow of naval officers had been trained as pilots since the mid-'20s, providing continuity while numbers were made up by RAF officers serving two-year tours between land-based 'postings'. A number of rating pilots (equivalent to US Navy enlisted pilots) were also trained, and there were four or five in each fighter squadron.

The decision to return the 'Fleet Air Arm' to the Navy had been taken in July 1937 – the 'Inskip Award' – and the two years which followed were taken up with the mechanical details of the transfer. Personnel proved to be a major problem: a few RAF pilots volunteered to transfer to the new 'Air Branch' and the Navy took the unprecedented step of offering short-service commissions to direct-entry aircrew. Britain was re-arming for a war which seemed ever more likely after 1937 and the Navy was thus in competition with the Air Force for suitable candidates, but sufficient applicants were accepted to be able to man the modest number of aircraft included in the expansion programme. When the Second World War began on 3rd September 1939, the Royal Navy had a total of 360 trained pilots and 332 under training – more than sufficient for the 232 front-line aircraft of all types but only just enough for the second-line and training units. There were only thirty-six fighters, in four squadrons.

Unfortunately, the Royal Navy could not increase its pilot strength unilaterally, like the other two navies, for one of the conditions of the Inskip Award had been that all Service flying training to Wings standard was to be undertaken by the Royal Air Force, at Elementary and Service Flying Training Schools, approximating to the US Navy's Basic and Intermediate Schools. A major disadvantage of the scheme was that the naval students were divorced from naval influence, other than that of a small naval staff, during the most formative months of their flying careers. Operational training was at naval schools, such as the RN Fighter School at Eastleigh near Southampton, until the summer of 1940 and thereafter at RN Air Station, Yeovilton, Somerset. The Fighter School was short of instructors with recent combat experience, as these were the pilots who were urgently needed to man the squadrons in action.

By the end of 1940, fifty pilots were leaving the operational training schools (fighter, torpedo-bomber, and catapult ship reconnaissance) every month, and there were 950 RN pilots with Wings, in the squadrons and at the schools. At this stage, the majority of the pre-Wings flying training of the RAF was being moved overseas, naval pilots going to Kingston, Ontario, Canada, where the airspace was less congested and less liable to occasional visits from the enemy. Rather more than 100 pilots per month were sent from Britain to Canada, but unfortunately the move coincided with a drop in the success rate, occasioned by a reduction in the standards required of pilot candidates. This reduced output came at a bad moment, for there was a sharp rise in combat casualties during the first half of 1941, so that on 1st July there were only 940 pilots in naval units.

This proved to be the nadir of the Navy's fortunes. In July, the first thirty students left for Pensacola, to be trained as fighter pilots by the US Navy, under a scheme first suggested by Vice Admiral J. H. Towers USN, Chief of the Bureau of Aeronautics. Thirty pilots joined Pensacola every month for the next year, and then the intake increased to fifty, a proportion being trained as torpedo-bomber pilots. By this time, the Royal Navy was inducting 195 pilots per month for training in Canada and the USA.

At the outbreak of the Pacific War, a large number of Canadian and New Zealand volunteers had come forward, only to find that their own Air Forces were too small to absorb them, but that the Royal Navy had recruiting officers seeking would-be aircrew. This new source of manpower allowed the Navy to tighten up its selection process, and the training wastage was reduced accordingly. By July 1942, there were 1,632 pilots with naval Wings, over 200 of whom were in fighter squadrons. The Fighter School was now adequately staffed with pilots with combat experience, and the Navy had even been able to start a 'post-graduate' School of Naval Air Warfare, to teach the latest tactics and techniques to the fighter leaders. Whereas pilots had gone to join squadrons with barely 120 hours total flying time in the summer of 1941, the syllabus now called for about 180 hours for pilots trained in Canada and over 200 for 'Towers Scheme' graduates, not including the ten-week operational training course.

The result was a large increase in the number of fighter squadrons in 1943: in September, there were 392 aircraft and pilots in formed units, compared with 247 a year earlier. Combat losses were low, and the number of pilots available to the Navy rose from 2,357 at the end of June 1943 to 3,343 in December. The peak monthly intake was reached during this period – 285 would-be pilots – but in order to reach this figure the educational standard had had to be lowered again. Wastage had stood at a constant 26 per cent of the total number beginning training, and this number stood steady until the end of 1943, but the average rose to 36 per cent during the opening months of 1944 – eighty-five students were being failed every month out of an intake of 250!

The 'Towers Scheme' trainees were not dropping out at such a high rate, thanks to the grading system used by the US Navy. The Royal Navy therefore adopted this careful pre-entry sifting, which necessarily reduced the number of applicants accepted. The manpower situation in Britain and the Dominions was such that by mid-1944 there were relatively few suitable candidates, although the RAF had reduced the level of its recruiting. The RAF was asked to provide 360 pilots from its surplus, and over 300 trained volunteers transferred to the Navy before the end of 1944, most of them being sent to the two Naval Fighter Schools.

Yeovilton and the new Fighter School at nearby Henstridge produced 100 fighter pilots between them every month from September 1944, when there

From 1942, the Royal Navy's Fighter School was equipped with ex-RAF Spitfires, as well as with Hurricanes, Fulmars and Martlets. Here, two Spitfire IIs formate on a Hurricane I of 759 Squadron. (*R. C. Jones*)

were 622 fighter aircraft in front-line service. The high rate of combat attrition and losses due to accident during the following nine months – 434 naval aircrew were killed or taken prisoner – and the need to form new squadrons and give rest tours to the pilots already in front-line squadrons reduced the net gain to about thirty pilots per month. With the Far East and Pacific becoming the Royal Navy's main combat theatres, there was an inevitable lag between the 'spare' pilots leaving the Fighter Schools and joining the fighter pool: up to ninety fighter pilots could be 'lost' in transit at a time, and the shortage of pilots plagued the British Pacific Fleet throughout 1945.

The last 'Towers Scheme' students arrived at Pensacola at the end of April 1945, and it was planned that thereafter seventy-eight pilots per month would go to Canada. The end of the war in Europe in May 1945 led to an immediate reduction in the RAF's flying training organisation, but provision was made for the transfer of 1,400 RAF, Australian, Canadian and New Zealand Air Force pilots to the Navy. In August 1945, the Royal Navy had 3,243 fully-trained pilots, as well as nearly 1,300 under-

going operational training and over 2,500 at the various pre-Wings stages.

The aircrew who entered during the war served as ratings until they completed training to Wings standard. Thereafter most pilots were commissioned as Midshipmen or Sub Lieutenants (Air) in the Royal Naval Volunteer Reserve (RNVR). A few fighter pilots remained non-commissioned, serving as Petty or Chief Petty Officers.

Due to the perpetual shortage of experienced pilots, promotion could be very swift. A Sub Lieutenant would serve approximately two years in the rank – the length of a front-line tour and a rest tour – before being promoted to Lieutenant. Depending upon ability and leadership qualities, he might be promoted to Acting Lieutenant Commander within six months. By the end of the war, the majority of the fighter squadron Commanding Officers were RNVR(A) Lieutenant Commanders who had first seen action in the summer and autumn of 1942 and the Fighter Wing Leaders were Air Branch Officers who had joined the Navy in 1938 and 1939 and had survived the bitter fighting of 1940 and 1941.

Sub Lieutenant R. H. Reynolds uses a portable radio to give advice to new pilots practising 'dummy deck landings' at a naval air station in Australia. (*G. Dennison*)

41

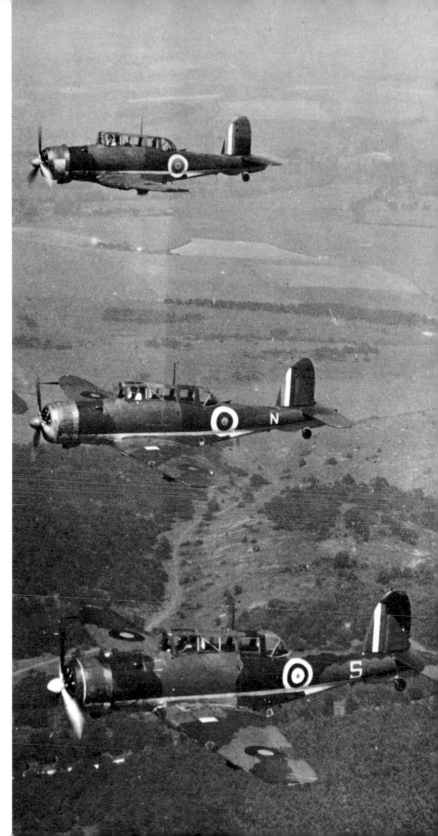

The workhorse of
the Norway
campaign. Few
photographs exist of
the Skua in action,
or, indeed, of carriers
during this period
(*R. C. Jones*)

4. Defensive

First Victory At the outbreak of war, on 3rd September 1939, the Royal Navy possessed two operational fighter squadrons in Home Waters – 800 and 803, both armed with Skuas and serving aboard *Ark Royal*. A third squadron, 801, was working-up with Skuas, with which it was to embark in *Furious* in October.

The first combats occurred on 26th September 1939, when *Ark Royal* was in the North Sea, some 250 miles north-west of Heligoland. No fighters were airborne when the first German shadower was sighted, and 15 minutes elapsed before the first sub-section of three aircraft was 'scrambled'. A second shadower appeared nearly an hour after the first had been driven off, damaged, and the sub-section of 803 Squadron launched to intercept this aircraft forced it down on to the water, the crew responsible being Lieutenant B. S. McEwen and his gunner, Petty Officer B. M. Seymour. The third enemy aircraft to appear was damaged and driven away by an 800 Squadron patrol.

The Dornier Do 18 flying-boats engaged by the Skuas had been flying at very low level, where their camouflage had been particularly effective under the overcast sky, and the Skuas had to be directed on to them, the carrier using visual signal lights and morse Wireless-Telegraphy – a long-winded process which resulted in minutes-old information being passed to the pilots. Unfortunately for the Skuas, the Do 18 was powered by Diesel engines and could therefore absorb many hits without catching fire, only the crew and controls being vulnerable to 0.303 in fire.

Although the shadowers had been driven away, they had still been able to pass position reports and six hours after the first had been seen *Ark Royal* was attacked by five Heinkel He 111 bombers. The Skuas were all in the hangars, their fuel tanks drained in anticipation of air attack, which was to be beaten off by the Fleet's anti-aircraft fire! Four bombers released from 6,000 feet and the fifth pressed in to release a 2,205 lb bomb from only 1,500 feet, the bomb missing by only 30 yards.

The Admiralty was not pleased with the results of the combat, or with the defensive policy adopted. Fleet commanders were instructed to use their fighters for defence against air attack, even if only for deterrent effect. On a higher level, their Lordships demanded the provision of Fleet fighter versions of the Hawker Hurricane and Supermarine Spitfire interceptors. Design work began on a folding-wing Spitfire and by the end of January 1940 it was expected that the first aircraft would be ready for carrier trials in October. The project was abandoned on the orders of Winston

The first British fighter victory of the war – a Dornier Do 18D forced down on the North Sea on 26th September, 1939. The crew of four were rescued by a British destroyer, which then sank the shadower with gunfire. (*MOD(N)*)

Churchill, and the Navy had to wait until 1941 before it received its first Sea Hurricanes and until mid-1942 before the Seafire entered service.

The Skuas of 800 and 803 Squadrons saw combat from shore bases, defending the Home Fleet base of Scapa Flow in the Orkneys during the winter and early spring of 1940. In five days of fighting, the Skuas drove off a score of Heinkel He 111s and Dornier Do 17s, but as the bombers were faster than the fighters once they had jettisoned their bombs, the only success claimed was a He 111 probably destroyed by Lieutenant W. P. Lucy, commanding 803 Squadron. A Roc turret-fighter of the same squadron damaged another He 111, the first of that fighter's few successes.

Norway — 1940

On 9th April 1940, German forces invaded Norway and Denmark. The Royal Navy's Home Fleet sailed on the same day but only one carrier, *Furious*, was available, *Ark Royal* being in the Mediterranean. *Furious'* fighter squadron, 801, was disembarked at the time, and for some reason it was decided that the Skuas could not join in time, so that the Fleet was left without fighters for the first critical fortnight of the campaign. That little assistance could be expected from the Royal Air Force's fighters was demonstrated on the evening of 9th April, when the Fleet was attacked by aircraft and a destroyer sunk and two light cruisers damaged by bombs. With no fighter cover, the heavy units had to leave the south-western sector of the Norwegian coast to be patrolled by submarines.

The shore-based Skua squadrons could reach the Norwegian coast and on 10th April twelve aircraft of 800 and 803 Squadrons dive-bombed and sank the light cruiser *Königsberg* at Bergen. On the same day, 'Crisis Gladiators' of 804 Squadron, also based in the Orkneys, joined RAF

44

Hurricanes in repulsing a 60-aircraft bomber raid on Scapa Flow, destroying one He 111 and damaging three other bombers. Six days later, on 16th April, 803 and 801 Squadrons patrolled over the damaged heavy cruiser *Suffolk* and destroyed a Do 17, damaged a Do 18, three He 111s, and a Junkers Ju 88, and drove off more bombers seeking to complete the destruction of *Suffolk*.

Ark Royal and *Glorious* arrived at Scapa Flow on 21st April and sailed on 23rd with eighteen Sea Gladiators, thirty Skuas and five Rocs, of 800, 801, 802, 803 and 804 Squadrons embarked, as well as eighteen Gladiators of No 263 Squadron RAF, the last to be disembarked to a frozen lake near Namsos, one of the two Allied toeholds in central Norway which were to be supported by the carrier force. The Sea Gladiators of 802 and 804, aboard *Glorious*, would be responsible for Fleet defence, while the Skua squadrons would undertake strikes and fighter patrols over the coast. Neither of the carriers was fitted with radar, but the force was accompanied by the cruiser *Curlew*, which possessed an 80-mile range Type 79 radar. With no fighter direction organisation, she had to pass bearings, ranges and estimated heights to the carriers, which would then 'instruct', rather than 'direct', the fighters. The first successful radar-controlled interception at sea occurred on the evening of 23rd April, when six Skuas were scrambled to damage a He 111 and drive off two more bombers.

The carrier force arrived off Aandalsnes on 24th April, flew off the RAF Gladiators, and then launched twelve Skuas to patrol over the town, 220 miles from the ships. 803 Squadron from *Glorious* met a raid over Aandalsnes and destroyed two He 111s and damaged a Do 17. One Skua was hit by return fire from a bomber and had to make a forced-landing ashore.

The Skuas turned their attentions to the Luftwaffe bases in the Trondheim area on the next day, and in co-operation with *Ark Royal's* Swordfish, they destroyed twelve bombers and reconnaissance aircraft, for the loss of four Skuas which were unable to find *Glorious* on return. The enemy were not distracted sufficiently to prevent the frozen lake base from being bombed and all the Air Force fighters were lost. The carriers were therefore obliged to turn their attentions to defensive patrols over Aandalsnes on 26th April, and eighteen Skua sorties resulted in eight interceptions, with a score of two He 111s destroyed and three damaged, for the loss of one Skua of 803 Squadron. The pilot of this aircraft, Lieutenant C. H. Filmer, survived, but his gunner, Petty Officer Baldwin, was killed – the first Royal Navy fighter crewman to be lost in action.

Another casualty of the same combat was Petty Officer J. Hadley, an 800 Squadron rating pilot, who was wounded in the face. The Skua lacked an armoured windscreen as well as any protection for its fuel tank – an unfortunate omission in a fighter committed to low-deflection stern attacks through its lack of speed. The poor hitting power of its four 0.303 in guns forced the pilots to get close to obtain results, and more casualties were to follow during the campaign. However, as experience in the combat use of the guns and the reflector sight was gained, so the effectiveness of the Skuas mounted.

The Sea Gladiators did not see sufficient action for their pilots to be able to 'learn on the job'. The first interception by 804 Squadron occurred on

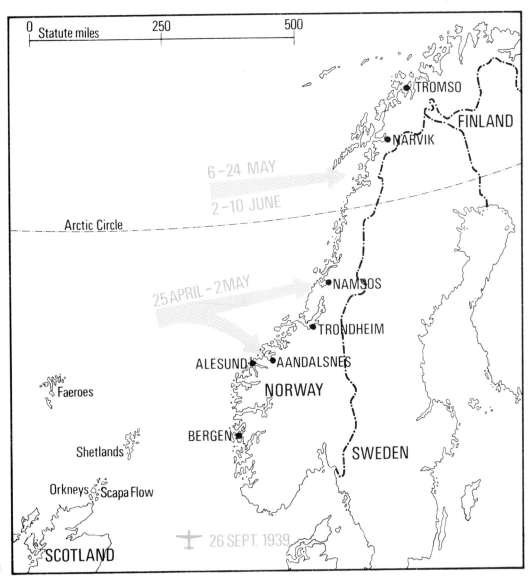

Norway 1940.

27th April, when Lieutenant R. M. Smeeton and his sub-section damaged an He 111 shadower which escaped at sea level, touching the sea three times as it made off, faster than the fighters could follow.

The Aandalsnes Skua patrols had their most successful day on 27th, destroying nine bombers and seriously damaging at least two others. The patrols led by Lieutenant E. G. D. Finch-Noyes of 800 Squadron, and Lieutenant Commander H. P. Bramwell, commanding 801, destroyed five of the enemy and drove off over twenty, making dummy attacks when all front and rear gun ammunition had been exhausted. Two Skuas were lost, but one crew was rescued. The following day saw further success – only six sorties were provided, but Lieutenant Lucy's and Lieutenant Finch-Noyes' sections destroyed three He 111s, a Ju 88, and damaged two Ju 88s and nine He 111s. The Rocs of 801 Squadron had their first airing on 28th April, being used to drive off shadowers detected by the modern light cruiser *Sheffield*, which had relieved *Curlew* as radar guard.

Glorious had left the force at dusk on 27th April, in order to refuel and to collect replacements for the lost fighters, rejoining on 30th. On 29th and 30th April, *Ark Royal* withdrew to the area of the Faeroe Islands, to rest her tired pilots and to escape the attentions of the Luftwaffe, which had by now located the carriers' operating area. As the force closed the Norwegian coast on 1st May, shadowers appeared once again and were unsuccessfully pursued by Sea Gladiators. One such chase distracted the radar operators aboard the new guardship, the battleship *Valiant*, and six Junkers Ju 87 'Stukas' made an unnoticed approach and attack, missing *Glorious* by 30 yards. A second wave was seen and intercepted by Lieutenant Smeeton – the Ju 87s jettisoned their bombs and dived away from the fighters. Three hours later, 802 Squadron claimed its first victim, Lieutenant J. F. Marmont following six Ju 87s into their dive and destroying one. The remaining dive-bombers pressed on in spite of the attentions of other fighters and again *Glorious* was near-missed.

The Commander-in-Chief, Home Fleet now ordered the carriers to withdraw, as the enemy now had U-boats in the area, as well as bombers which could clearly get through. Namsos and Aandalsnes were therefore evacuated without the benefit of air cover, but in spite of heavy air attacks the only casualties were two destroyers.

Ark Royal returned to operate alone off Narvik on 6th May. The Luftwaffe bases were too distant for the enemy to be able to make large-scale raids, but the Skuas nevertheless destroyed six assorted enemy aircraft, damaged eight more, and engaged and drove off another eighteen, in the course of sixteen days consecutive operations. Five Skuas were shot down, but the only crew lost was Lieutenant Lucy and his Observer, Lieutenant M. C. E. Hanson, who were shot down in flames by an He 111 on 14th May. Commanding 803 Squadron, Lucy had led his sub-section to destroy six enemy aircraft and had damaged five others – all He 111s.

The Skuas had two noteworthy combats, both on 16th May. While on patrol over Narvik, Lieutenant L. A. Harris (a Royal Marines officer) and Petty Officer A. H. Glover of 803 Squadron saw what they thought to be two Do 17 bombers below them and promptly attacked, only to have another pair of 'Do 17s' descend upon them. Although the Skua pilots did not realise it, their opponents were in fact Messerschmitt Bf 110C twin-engined fighters, which out-performed and out-manoeuvred the Skuas in a 30-minute dog-fight. The carrier fighters tried to lure the enemy within range of the Narvik ships' AA guns but before this could be achieved Harris was shot down (and rescued), but Glover's gunner, Naval Airman S. G. Wright, evened the score by shooting one of the enemy down. The Bf 110s had come from the *Zerstörer Staffel* of *Kampfgruppe 30*, which also possessed a flight of Ju 88 fighters. All six of the Ju 88s were encountered by another 803 patrol, led by Lieutenant J. M. Christian. After so

Lieutenant
B. Paterson
(shirtsleeves) and his
'Flight' with Sea
Gladiator 'G' of 804
Squadron. In the
cockpit is Sub
Lieutenant W. E. G.
Taylor, RN, an
American citizen
who had joined the
'Air Branch' before
the outbreak of war.
(Mod(N))

many frustrating chases after so many Ju 88s, the Skua pilots were delighted to meet an enemy who would stay and fight and two were promptly destroyed, at no cost to 803 Squadron.

RAF fighters flew ashore to defend the Narvik area from 22nd May, Gladiators being delivered by *Furious* and Hurricanes by *Glorious*. A day or two after the latter had arrived, the decision was taken to evacuate Narvik and *Ark Royal* and *Glorious* returned, the one to cover the evacuation and the other to take off the remaining RAF fighters. Bad weather prevented the Luftwaffe from interfering seriously with the operation, and it was not until 8th June that *Ark's* Skuas had to drive off a shadower. On the same day, *Glorious* was sunk by the German battlecruisers *Gneisenau* and *Scharnhorst;* one of the two destroyers screening the carrier managed to torpedo *Scharnhorst* before the 11-inch guns finished both off.

The damaged battlecruiser put in to Trondheim for emergency repairs while *Ark Royal* covered the Narvik convoys against possible attack. One He 111 bomber was shot down and two more damaged on 9th June – technically this was a night interception, but in such northerly latitudes it was barely twilight at midnight, giving the carrier a 24-hour air defence problem. Once the convoys were beyond the reach of the enemy, *Ark Royal* headed for Trondheim to attack *Scharnhorst*,

Bad weather prevented a strike from being launched until midnight on 12th/13th June, by which time the naval force had been waiting for thirty-six hours, sighted from time to time by reconnaissance aircraft. With the example of *Königsberg* of the effectiveness of the Skuas, the Germans had had time to prepare for the strike, but the situation was made worse by an RAF attack on the Vaernes airfield. This raid, by four Beauforts, was intended to be co-ordinated with the Skua attack, but it was delivered too early, in insufficient strength, and served only to stir up the Messerschmitt Bf 109s and 110s. Six Blenheim long-range fighters should have protected the Skuas, but these arrived late, and the bomb-laden naval aircraft were harried before, during and after their attack, which scored only one hit. Eight out of the fifteen Skuas were shot down, the casualties including the Commanding Officers of 800 and 803 Squadrons, and Lieutenants Finch-Noyes and Filmer. One Bf 110 was damaged by both the pilot and the gunner of one of the surviving Skuas.

Experienced replacements were found for the lost leaders, but the Royal Navy's slender reserve of fighter crews was cut to the point where another such debacle would prejudice the modest expansion programme.

The Norwegian campaign has been covered in greater detail than any other carrier deployment as every aspect of Second World War Fleet fighter operations was exercised. The Skuas, Rocs and Sea Gladiators defended their own task force and Skuas alone defended convoys and Allied troops ashore. Offensively, the Skuas were used for strikes on enemy air bases and shipping, and for close support in the Narvik area.

For this first major naval operation of the war, the Royal Navy deployed a balanced carrier task force, with two carriers supported by cruisers for AA defence and destroyers as an anti-submarine screen. A radar equipped ship was at all times in company to act as an air-raid warning guard. For the initial operations, off Aandalsnes and Trondheim, the Royal Navy committed all five of its operational fighter squadrons and the reinforcements received by *Ark Royal* on 30th April consisted of all the aircraft allocated to a sixth squadron, scheduled to commission on 1st May. The older *Glorious* was not included in the Narvik task force as her radius of action was insufficient for prolonged operations, but all three Skua squadrons were represented in *Ark Royal*, with twenty-seven aircraft between them.

The total commitment of the Royal Navy to the campaign was evidenced by its willingness to attempt to provide a substitute for land-based air power for days on end, always within range of enemy bombers and usually in waters known to be threatened by U-boats. Such persistence was not to be demonstrated again by the Royal Navy for three years: the strength of German air power and the inadequacy of the fighter defence made any operation lasting more than three days an almost suicidal venture.

There can be no doubt that off Norway the fighter defence provided by *Glorious* was not successful. The radar operators were inexperienced and the Sea Gladiators lacked the performance and fire-power to deal with the raiders – although slightly faster than the Skuas, their diving speed was low and enemy aircraft could easily leave them behind by evading. Nevertheless, experience of defensive tactics was gained, although the carriers were fortunate in escaping unscathed from the attacks which got through.

The success of the Skuas was somewhat surprising. Although faster than the German reconnaissance floatplanes and flying boats, they were vastly outperformed by the German medium bombers, with the exception of the fully-loaded Heinkel He 111 – once the latter jettisoned its bombs then it too could leave a Skua at the same height far behind. At first, the Skua pilots achieved few kills, but as they gained experience, they learned to use their high diving speed to catch the bombers and the shooting of pilots and gunners improved so that the first pass inflicted damage which slowed the enemy to a speed within the Skuas' reach. The first sure sign that the fighter pilots were gaining the ascendancy came on 27th April, when nine bombers were shot down and over a score of others damaged or driven off. It was ironic that the Army commander ashore should comment on this day that 'our air was conspicuous by its absence'.

Ark Royal could never hope to provide a watertight cover in the face of overwhelming enemy air superiority – later experience with carriers operating fifteen times as many fighters was to show that a really determined enemy could nearly always defeat the system – but her aircraft undoubtedly reduced the weight of bombs dropped on the ill-fated expeditionary forces in Central and Northern Norway. The Germans learned a new respect for the carrier and its fighters: the Luftwaffe's lack of experience in locating and attacking ships at sea led to fresh emphasis being put upon the training of a specialist anti-shipping force – the *Fliegerkorps X* which was to dominate the Central Mediterranean in early 1941.

On the other hand, the Royal Navy was considerably chastened by its experiences off Norway. It was realised that not only the Skua but also the Fairey Fulmar, which had not yet entered service, were not capable of carrying out the unexpected task of taking on the Luftwaffe for days on end. The enemy would not continue to miss the carriers when the latter were exposed to sustained attacks. Until a better interceptor could be provided, the carriers were not to be exposed to air attack except under circumstances of extreme strategic urgency.

Mediterranean Convoys — 1941

The 'circumstances of extreme strategic urgency' arose within a year of the end of the Norwegian campaign. Before the latter had drawn to its sad close, the German Army had broken through the Allied defensive lines and encircled the Armies which had to be evacuated from Dunkirk. Italy joined the war on 10th June but made little contribution to the fall of France two weeks later. The Royal Navy filled the gap left in the western Mediterranean by the formation of Force 'H', which included *Ark Royal*, at Gibraltar at the end of June 1940. At the other end of the Mediterranean, protecting Egypt and the Suez Canal, the Alexandria-based Mediterranean Fleet included the carrier *Eagle*, which did not have a fighter squadron, but which embarked three Sea Gladiators left behind by *Glorious*.

The Mediterranean Fleet was shadowed and attacked by Italian aircraft virtually every time it put to sea. The Sea Gladiators, flown by Swordfish pilots, enjoyed a measure of success against the Savoia-Marchetti SM.79 medium-level bombers which were as fast as the fighters but less well protected than the German bombers. Only once did the fighters

intercept one of the skilful and tenacious shadowers, the Captain of *Eagle* preferring to keep his aircraft in hand until the bombers approached. No radar guardship was available, but in the clear air of the Mediterranean sufficient warning could often be given by alert visual look-outs, particularly as the Italian bombers were wont to work round to a favourable sector for attack in full view of the intended targets.

Eagle was joined at the beginning of September 1940 by the new armoured carrier *Illustrious*, the first carrier to be fitted with radar and the first to carry the eight-gun Fairey Fulmar. For four months, the fifteen Fulmars of 806 Squadron enjoyed total air supremacy, destroying and damaging over forty Italian aircraft. On occasion, the weight of fire delivered in the first pass by a section was so effective that shadowers, taken by surprise, were destroyed before they could report the Fleet. At the other end of the Mediterranean, *Ark Royal* embarked the Fulmars of 808 in place of 803 Squadron's Skuas. Force 'H' was not used quite so aggressively as the Mediterranean Fleet and the lack of opportunity, coupled with *Ark Royal's* lack of radar, resulted in the fighters being less obviously successful.

Illustrious' reign came to an end on 10th January 1941. The Regia Aeronautica had made many unsuccessful attempts to hit her from high level, combined with occasional torpedo attacks, but the Luftwaffe achieved success at the first attempt. *Fliegerkorps X*, *Ark Royal's* opposition off Norway, moved to Sicily at the beginning of January 1941 as part of the overall German plan for assisting the flagging Italian ally, but with the specific task of sinking the carrier. *Illustrious* was 55 miles to the west of Malta, supporting a convoy, when a pair of SM.79 torpedo-bombers drew the four Fulmars on patrol down to sea level, dropped their torpedoes ineffectively, and were then pursued to a distance of 20 miles. Two of the fighters had expended all their ammunition but neither SM.79 had been

Sea Gladiator of 813 Squadron's fighter flight lands aboard HMS *Eagle* in the Mediterranean during the summer of 1940. (*via R. C. Jones*)

51

shot down, and at this point *Illustrious* detected an incoming raid, 30 miles distant at 12,000 feet. The winded patrol far away in the opposite direction had no chance of intercepting and nor did the four Fulmars scrambled after detection. The Ju 87Rs attacked opposed only by AA gunfire and scored six hits on the carrier, failing to sink her but putting her out of action for a year. She had been the victim of poor defensive technique, allowing all of the Fulmars on patrol to chase a harmless enemy. Shadowers had been present for three and a half hours before the first attack – with Sicily only 65 miles away from the carrier and convoy, a heavier scale of attack was only to be expected.

Illustrious was replaced by *Formidable* in March 1941. The new carrier brought the twelve Fulmars of 803 Squadron, which was joined by the survivors of 806 Squadron. The shortage of naval fighter aircraft in the eastern Mediterranean was acute, and the available strength of the two squadrons seldom exceeded eighteen aircraft. In April 1941, 807 Squadron replaced 800 Squadron in *Ark Royal*, so that ship also possessed two Fulmar squadrons: availability was low, for although the supply line to Gibraltar was shorter, the base lacked the second-line workshop facilities to be found in Egypt.

In May 1941, both ships played a major role in Operation 'Tiger' – a fast convoy carrying tanks and aircraft through the Mediterranean to the hard-pressed British 8th Army, driven back into Egypt by General Rommel's Afrika Korps. *Ark Royal* and Force 'H' picked up the convoy as it passed through the Straits of Gibraltar on 6th May. On the same day, the Mediterranean Fleet left Alexandria to head for a rendezvous to the south of Malta.

Both forces, and the convoy, remained undetected until 8th May, thanks to generally poor weather and bad visibility, which persisted throughout the operation. In spite of having only twelve Fulmars fit for operations, *Ark Royal* maintained two two-aircraft sections on patrol from 0800 on 8th, as the convoy began to enter the 100-mile wide channel between Sardinia and Algeria. A shadower sighted the convoy and escaped into cloud at about noon, and two hours later the cruiser *Sheffield*, the radar guard and fighter direction ship, detected a raid 32 miles distant. Both Fulmar sections airborne intercepted the enemy, who consisted of sixteen SM.79 torpedo-bombers, escorted by twelve Fiat CR.42 biplane fighters. The escort immediately bounced the interceptors, shooting down the Commanding Officer of 808 Squadron, and although a number of SM.79s turned back, eight broke through unmolested and came close to torpedoing *Ark Royal* and the battlecruiser *Renown*. Out-performed and out-manoeuvred by the more numerous CR.42s, the Fulmars had had little chance to get at the bombers and three hours later the experience was repeated, but again the SM.79s missed *Ark Royal*.

The convoy came within reach of the Luftwaffe bases in Sicily about an hour before dusk, and a raid was promptly detected 70 miles away. Three Fulmars were airborne and another four were flown off to patrol 15 miles from the convoy at medium level; the seven fighters were the only ones serviceable at the time. The enemy, twenty-eight Ju 87s in two formations, with a top cover of six Bf 110s, were sighted about 20 miles from the convoy and all three sections attacked, three aircraft of 808 Squadron taking

By November 1940, HMS *Illustrious* was so short of Fulmars that two Sea Gladiators had to be embarked to make up numbers in 806 Squadron for the Taranto strike operation. On 8th November, Lt O. J. R. Nicholls led the two biplanes to destroy a Cant Z.501 flying-boat shadower. (*J. M. Phillips*)

Left.
From October 1940 until April 1941, HMS *Ark Royal* operated the Fulmars of 807 Squadron and the Skuas of 800 Squadron side by side, the latter being retained primarily for their strike capability. (*IWM A3735*)

A Cant Z.1007*bis* crashes inside the Fleet's screen after being hit by Fulmar gunfire.

on the Messerschmitts while a pair from each of 807 and 808 Squadron bounced the 'Stukas'. The result was a convincing victory for the aggressive Fulmar pilots, who shattered the dive-bomber formations, sending enemy aircraft in all directions to seek cover in cloud. One Ju 87 was destroyed and three damaged, and one Bf 110 was damaged. Three Fulmars were slightly damaged by return fire from rear-firing guns. The carrier and heavy ships

of Force 'H' turned back at dusk, leaving the convoy to pass through the Sicilian Narrows under cover of darkness.

To the east of Malta, *Formidable's* fighters were dealing with Luftwaffe shadowers in a summary fashion, destroying three He 111s and damaging a Ju 88, as well as disposing of an Italian Cant Z.1007*bis*. The effect of these losses, and several narrow escapes, was to force the Greece-based Luftwaffe shadowers to maintain touch at greater heights, where they were faster than the Fulmars, and to approach and depart at even greater heights, where the Fulmars could not reach them at all.

The convoy was cloaked by bad weather for its daylight passage to join *Formidable* and the Fleet to the south of Malta, but the carrier's fighters destroyed a Sicily-based Ju 88 on 9th May. The enemy lost touch for over 24 hours, but in the afternoon of 10th, the shadowers took up station once again. Not until the afternoon of 11th May did a raid actually approach the convoy, but this, by nine Ju 88s, was intercepted by an 806 Squadron section which had already accounted for two Ju 88s during the operation – Lieutenant R. S. Henley and Sub Lieutenant P. D. J. Sparke. Henley damaged his target, but Sparke destroyed his by closing in to 20 yards; sadly, Sparke's Fulmar was hit by return fire and he and his telegraphist were killed. This was the last combat of 'Tiger', which had cost the enemy ten aircraft destroyed by Fulmars, and as many damaged, for the loss of four Fulmars. One of the merchant ships had been sunk by mine off Tunisia, but the remaining five landed 238 tanks and forty-three Hurricanes at Alexandria, three weeks earlier than would have been possible had they been sent by the safer route around Africa.

A damaged Fulmar is hung over *Ark Royal's* port deck edge to clear the deck for the recovery of other aircraft. The patches over three of the wing guns have been shot away, suggesting that the Fulmar has been in recent combat. (*via C. F. Shores*)

55

A Junkers Ju 87R 'Stuka' is chased by a *Formidable* Fulmar after the bombing of the carrier off Crete in May 1941. (*J. M. Phillips*)

Formidable was damaged off Crete within the month. Only twelve serviceable Fulmars were aboard when she was sent to attack a Luftwaffe bomber base in an attempt to reduce the enemy weight of attack on the naval forces evacuating the island. The Fulmars strafed the airfield, destroyed two and drove off five shadowers, but were unable to prevent Ju 88s and Ju 87s, escorted by Bf 110s, from hitting the carrier. It may have seemed to be folly to attempt offensive operations under the circumstances, but the Royal Navy had its obligations to the soldiers leaving Crete, and as the Commander-in-Chief, Mediterranean Fleet, is reported to have commented, 'A ship can be built in three years, but it takes three hundred years to rebuild a tradition!'

Formidable departed without replacement so that the Mediterranean Fleet was thereafter unable to provide its own air cover for Malta supply convoys. The RAF in Egypt lacked the means to supply land-based air protection against Luftwaffe bombers based in Greece and Crete. The three naval fighter squadrons serving ashore in Egypt were used to protect coastal convoys, or misemployed in support of land operations over the Desert. Two major convoys were run to Malta during the second half of 1941, but both came from the west, escorted from Gibraltar to the Sicilian Channel by Force 'H'.

Ark Royal was at sea and in action between 23rd and 25th July, protecting the Operation 'Substance' convoy. There were three engagements with bomber raids as well as the usual driving off of shadowers. The first attack was met by no fewer than eleven Fulmars, out of the twenty-one available, and although the fighters intercepted at 20 miles from the convoy, the SM.79 medium-level bombers were travelling almost as fast as the Fulmars, which managed to shoot down only two SM.79s and severely damaged two others. Three Fulmars were shot down, but five of the survivors then clim-

Lieutenant D. C. E. F. Gibson, who scored victories while flying Skuas, Fulmars and Martlets, seen with the wreckage of a Vichy French Morane MS.406C shot down during the Syrian campaign in June 1941. (*Vice Admiral Gibson*)

HMS *Ark Royal* scrambles five Fulmars during Operation 'Substance' – the July 1941 Malta convoy (*J. C. Woods*)

After the damaging of *Formidable*, the carrier-less 803 and 806 Squadrons flew RAF Hurricanes from airfields in Egypt and Libya. Re-armed with Fulmars in February 1942, the two squadrons were transferred to Ceylon shortly before the Japanese carriers attacked the island. (*Vice Admiral Gibson*)

bed to their maximum of 15,000 feet to intercept a formation of Z.1007*bis*, which were forced to bomb wide of the ships, even though the fighters could not reach within 1,000 feet of their height. While these medium-level activities were distracting the defences, seven torpedo-bombers made a surprise attack at low level, sinking a destroyer and damaging a light cruiser. Two more SM.79s were destroyed out of a small group of torpedo-bombers intercepted 25 miles away on the afternoon of 23rd.

Two days later, to the south of Sardinia, two 808 Squadron sections, led by Lieutenants A. T. J. Kindersley and E. D. G. Lewin, intercepted and broke up a formation of about twenty bombers, destroying four and damaging two for the loss of Kindersley and his Observer, and the Fulmar (only) of his wingman, Lieutenant J. C. Cockburn.

The growing number of Fulmars lost to return fire was due in part to the improved armour protection being fitted to Italian bombers and reconnaissance aircraft – one Cant Z.506B floatplane had been shot down and two damaged, at the cost of one Fulmar – and also to the Fulmar's lack of frontal protection, for the pilot and coolant system. Eight 0.303 in machine guns were inadequate for combat in 1941, the lack of penetration of the light round forcing the fighters to close to point-blank range to inflict serious damage. 'De Wilde' explosive incendiary ammunition was available, but could not provide the 'punch' needed, and which could only be provided by a 0.50 in machine gun or 20 mm cannon. The Fulmar had an armoured windscreen and an armoured fuel tank behind the pilot, but its frontally-mounted radiator was vulnerable to gunfire: even a small-calibre hit could lead to an engine coolant leak, resulting in engine overheating and fire.

Ark Royal was offered three Sea Hurricanes in July 1941. Old ex-RAF aircraft, the single-seaters were barely capable of 300 mph at 18,000 feet, and although they had the same armament as the Fulmars, they had only half the ammunition capacity and less than half the patrol endurance. Comparative trials showed that the Fulmar II's performance below 10,000 feet was rather better than the Hurricane's, and so although the latter

would have been useful for patrols above the Fulmar's ceiling, the carrier declined the offer.

Meanwhile, RAF Hurricanes were being taken to sea by *Ark Royal* and other carriers. These aircraft were ferried to a position some 500 miles west of Malta and then flown off to the island – 290 of them in nine operations in 1941.

For her last Malta convoy, Operation 'Halberd', *Ark Royal* embarked no fewer than twenty-seven Fulmars of 807 and 808 Squadrons. At noon on 27th September 1941, when the convoy was some 90 miles south of Sardinia, the radar guardship detected a raid at low level, 30 miles distant, and eight patrolling Fulmars were vectored out to intercept. The carrier scrambled seven more fighters, steaming downwind at high speed to do so, but these did not engage the enemy before the torpedo-bombers reached the destroyer screen. Only six out of twelve Savoia-Marchetti SM.84s got past the first interception, which cost them one of their number, and the ships' AA fire and the Fulmars which had just taken off accounted for two more. Hardly had this attack died away, when a small group of SM.84s attacked without warning, scoring one hit on the battleship *Nelson*, but for the loss of two to AA fire and a third to fighters. A third wave, also of SM.84s, showed little inclination to close the convoy, only three even reaching a dropping position, where one was 'splashed' by Fulmars and another by AA. The ships' gun crews had had a field day, destroying four torpedo-bombers and, regrettably, two Fulmars. Having lost a third of the bombers which had pressed their attacks, subsequent Italian raids showed extreme caution, withdrawing as soon as Fulmars were sighted. It would appear that although the fighters lacked the firepower to destroy many bombers, they were inflicting heavy personnel casualties within the damaged bombers which returned to base.

Ark Royal was torpedoed and sunk in mid-November 1941, while returning from a Hurricane ferrying mission. Since 'Halberd' her fighters had destroyed three shadowers and damaged another for the loss of one Fulmar. The heyday of the Fulmar was over, for from the beginning of 1942

Ark Royal in the convoy 'box' during Operation 'Halberd', her last Malta convoy, in September 1941. (*IWM A5627*)

59

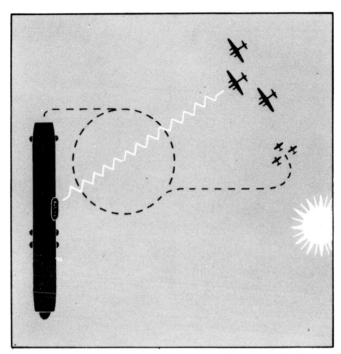

The Basic Radar-controlled Day Interception: by 1941, British Fighter Direction Officers had gained sufficient expeience to permit them to set up an interception, conning the fighters right on to an enemy, instead of vectoring the patrol from its holding position directly towards the threat. By directing the fighters to approach from the target's beam, down-sun if possible, the former did not have to make a time-consuming 180° turn in full view of the enemy and could go straight from the approach into their ¼-attacks.

single-seat fighters began to out-number them at sea. In the Mediterranean, four squadrons – 803, 806, 807, and 808 – had destroyed ninety and damaged over fifty German, Italian, and Vichy French aircraft, for the loss of twenty-three Fulmars. The best had been made of a mediocre fighter, by the use of radar direction techniques, which had allowed the limited number of fighters to be concentrated against raids. The low-level 'under-the-radar' approach by land-based torpedo-bombers was still causing occasional trouble, particularly when there were medium-level bombers about. Of particular value to the fighter direction officers was the 'Identification Friend/Foe' (IFF) equipment fitted in the fighters: triggered by an electronic signal from the ship, a simple transmitter in the aircraft broadcast a coded signal which was displayed on the radar screen, thus permitting the FDO to establish immediately the identity of his fighters – contacts not showing IFF were therefore probably hostile.

The Types 79 and 281 radar used by the Royal Navy had no panoramic (Plan Position) display at this stage, and the antennae had to be swung to cover a sector to establish the precise bearing and range of a contact, one ship thus tracking a raid while another kept an all-round search. To track the fighters continuously would have been wasteful of time, and they were therefore plotted by dead-reckoning and only brought on to the radar when in the vicinity of the enemy, when the FDO was setting up the ideal down-sun approach to a surprise quarter-attack. The ground rules for carrier task force defence were established during these 1941 convoy battles and the information was passed on to the United States Navy, which came into the war on 7th December 1941.

The Pacific — 1941-42

The six Imperial Japanese Navy carriers which attacked Oahu on 7th December 1941 were operating 135 Mitsubishi A6M2 'Zero-Sen' fighters. The US Pacific Fleet possessed only three carriers, with twenty-eight Grumman F4F-3 and 3As and twenty-seven Brewster F2A-3s. *Lexington's* Fighting Squadron (VF-) 2 was operating F2As, *Enterprise's* VF-6 had F4Fs, and *Saratoga's* VF-3 was re-arming with Grummans at San Diego. By great good fortune, none of the carriers was at Pearl Harbour when the Japanese struck.

Akagi, Kaga, Hiryu, Soryu, Zuikaku, and *Shokaku* each kept nine fighters back to provide fighter patrols over the force, with eighteen aircraft always on station and eighteen manned on deck at immediate readiness. The remainder of the A6Ms went with the strikes, forty-five in the first wave and thirty-six in the second. There was little airborne opposition over Oahu and the Japanese fighters made short work of the US Army Air Force interceptors which did manage to take-off. Many of the A6Ms of the first wave did not return with the torpedo and dive-bombers, but remained over the target areas to ensure complete air supremacy and to deny the air defences the respite needed to rally. Only five of the twenty-nine Japanese aircraft lost in combat were destroyed by the Curtiss P-36s and P-40s, twenty-two being destroyed by anti-aircraft fire.

The other two aircraft, both A6Ms, were destroyed by ship-borne aircraft. *Enterprise* was only 200 miles to the west of Oahu at the time of the attack, returning from a ferry operation which had delivered US Marine Corps F4Fs to Wake Island. Fifteen Douglas SBD-2 Dauntless dive-bombers of Scouting (VS-) 6 arrived during the semi-pause between the attack waves and three of the 250-mph Dauntlesses unhesitatingly took on Japanese fighters, destroying one but all being shot down in flames. A more improbable 'kill' was that scored by two Curtiss SOC-3 biplane spotters, each armed with one fixed and one free 0.30 in gun. The floatplanes, from the heavy cruiser *Northampton*, met a damaged A6M returning alone to its carrier and finished it off.

American carrier aircraft saw no further aerial combat until 1st February 1942, but the Japanese fighters were in action over Wake Island, Rabaul and New Guinea. Opposition was slight and the Japanese sustained no combat losses from Allied fighter action.

On 1st February 1942, the US Navy launched its first offensive missions against Japanese shore installations – airfields in the Gilbert and Marshall Islands and shipping at Kwajalein. *Enterprise* despatched eleven of her eighteen F4F-3s on fighter-bomber strikes against Maleolap and Wotje, where their 116-lb bombs inflicted little damage. The fighters had been fitted with improvised armour behind the pilot's seat during the previous month,

One of *Soryu's* 'Zeroes' takes off during the 'Hawaiian Operation'.

For the attack on Pearl Harbour, 49 of the 'Kates' were armed with 1,768 lb Type 99 armour-piercing bombs, converted from 16 in shells.

The only 'Claude' fighters to see action from carriers during the Pacific War were those operated by *Ryujo* and *Zuiho*, whose units did not receive 'Zeroes' until the end of the East Indies campaign.

Lieutenant Commander Takahashi's 'Val' approaches *Shokaku's* island during the take-off roll. The dive-bombers from this ship and *Zuikaku* attacked the Oahu airfields, leaving Pearl Harbour to the more experienced crews of the other four carriers.

and the presence of $\frac{3}{8}$-inch boiler plate undoubtedly saved one pilot from injury when his aircraft was hit by AA fire.

As the *Enterprise* force withdrew from the Marshalls during the afternoon a small Japanese raid was detected at a range of over 40 miles. Lack of experience on the part of the fighter direction officer resulted in a poor estimation of the enemy's height, and the F4F patrol was unable to find the seven Mitsubishi G4M 'Betty' bombers between layers of cloud. The G4Ms were all destroyed by AA and fighters during and after their attack, but one, hit by AA, tried to crash on the carrier, clipping the deck edge before hitting the sea.

Yorktown, to the south of the Marshalls, was not attacked, but her VF-42 was vectored out to destroy a Kawanishi H6K 'Mavis' flying-boat shadower. The carriers' FDOs complained of the total lack of IFF in their aircraft: identification required considerable R/T chatter and waste of time before the fighters could be sorted out from friendly strike and patrol aircraft, let alone from 'hostile' contacts. The poor R/T sets fitted to the F4Fs were a further cause of complaint. The High-Frequency radios were tunable to give an infinite choice of frequencies within the band, but both receiver and transmitter required tuning, and matching was difficult enough on the ground but virtually impossible for pilots in the air. Two-way radio contact could not be guaranteed outside 30 miles from the ship, thus depriving the defence of the benefits of long-range radar detection and the F4F's good endurance. The Royal Navy fighters were fitted with H/F sets with four push-button, pre-selected crystal-controlled frequencies, with a reliable range of up to 90 miles at 10,000 feet.

Three weeks after the Marshalls strikes, *Lexington* attempted to attack Rabaul, being built up as the enemy's main base in South-West Pacific area. The carrier and her screen were 300 miles from the target and 100 miles outside the maximum striking range of her aircraft when the first 'Mavis' shadower appeared and was promptly shot down by VF-3. Another followed three hours later, but a third escaped the fighters and reported the force. Eighteen G4M bombers took off from Rabaul, in two waves of nine.

The raid was detected by *Lexington's* CXAM radar at a range of 76 miles and the eight F4Fs on Combat Air Patrol (CAP) were vectored to meet the enemy at a range of 30 miles. The interception was completely successful although the bombers did manage to release their bombs near the carrier, which was launching more fighters. Unfortunately, six of the eight fighters airborne continued the pursuit until all of the bombers had been destroyed, leaving only two fighters at height to meet the second wave, known to be coming in. Lieutenant E. O'Hare was leading this section and after his wingman's guns jammed during the first pass he was left to deal with the enemy single-handed. Two were shot down before the gun defence was reached – thereafter the AA fire, bursting consistently astern of the enemy, effectively drove off the fighters, the newly-scrambled aircraft from *Lexington* having joined O'Hare. The 'Betties' failed to score any hits and six more were destroyed during their escape, three by O'Hare. Two F4Fs had fallen to the bombers' guns, hit in their unprotected fuel tanks while making passes from dead astern. With all hopes of surprise gone, the carrier strike was abandoned and the force withdrew without further incident.

Soryu prepares to fly off a deck load of 'Zeroes' and 'Vals' during operations off Java in late February 1942.

The US Navy's first ace – Lieutenant E. H. O'Hare of VF-3 in the F4F-3 in which he destroyed five 'Betties' on 20th February, 1942. (*USN 80-G-64833*)

On the previous day, 19th February, the Japanese carriers had enjoyed considerable success in a strike on Darwin, in northern Australia. Only ten US Army Air Force P-40C fighters were airborne to oppose 188 carrier aircraft, which included over 50 A6Ms. The P-40s, which had been attempting to fly to Timor and were thus present only through chance, managed to destroy one Japanese aircraft before they were themselves slaughtered by the 'Zeroes'.

Ceylon Free from any worries about interference from Australia, the Japanese carriers turned to seal off the Allies' escape route from Java, which was invaded on 1st March and fell on 9th March. After a restorative break from operations, taken at Staring Bay, Celebes, five large carriers sailed to attack the British bases in Ceylon and a light carrier left to clean up shipping in the Bay of Bengal. Aboard the six carriers were 117 A6Ms, 114 D3A 'Val' dive-bombers, and 146 B5N 'Kate' torpedo or level bombers

British naval fighter opposition to the Japanese carrier sortie into the Indian Ocean was provided by two Fulmar squadrons in Ceylon, the Fulmars of 800 Squadron and the Sea Hurricanes of 880 Squadron aboard *Indomitable* (above) and the Martlet IIs of *Formidable's* 888 Squadron (left) (*G. Wallace, D. R. Whittaker*)

– double the number of aircraft available to the Allied ship and shore-based units in Ceylon and India. The Royal Navy had assembled a powerful Fleet in the Indian Ocean, bearing in mind British naval commitments in the Mediterranean and Atlantic, but of the three carriers, *Hermes* carried only twelve biplane Swordfish torpedo-bombers, and the armoured carriers *Indomitable* and *Formidable* had only twenty-one serviceable fighters between them – six Grumman Martlet IIs, eight Fulmars, and eleven Sea Hurricanes – out of an authorised strength of thirty-seven which would still have been inadequate to defend the Fleet against the Japanese. Two Fulmar squadrons – 803 and 806 – were ashore in Ceylon, as well as forty-nine RAF Hurricane IIs which had been delivered by *Indomitable* in late February.

The Japanese task force was detected on 4th April, 415 miles to the south-east of Ceylon, but the lack of a long-range striking force meant that the island would have to take the first blow while the Eastern Fleet's carriers attempted to reach a position from which they could attack the enemy.

Colombo was attacked on 5th April. A radar station had recently been established nearby, but poor siting made it virtually useless and the thirty-three Hurricanes and Fulmars which made contact with the thirty-six A6Ms and eighty-nine bombers did so without the aid of ground controllers. Six D3As and a single A6M were shot down, but the Japanese aircraft destroyed twelve Hurricanes and four Fulmars, as well as six Swordfish torpedo-bombers found near Colombo. The RAF and naval pilots had made the mistake of trying to manoeuvre with the 'Zeroes', over-confident in the tactics which had proved effective against German and Italian aircraft.

The Japanese carriers withdrew after inflicting little serious damage on Colombo but sinking two heavy cruisers caught without fighter cover at sea. A Fairey Albacore reconnaissance aircraft from *Indomitable* sighted the enemy force, but the Eastern Fleet could not reach a suitable launching position for a night strike before the enemy was well clear, on its way to replenish prior to a further attack, on the Trincomalee naval base.

As at Colombo, warning was obtained on the day before the strike, so that most of the ships in harbour had been dispersed to sea. The radar station at Trincomalee had been operational for only two or three days, but the incoming raid on 9th April was detected at over 50 miles, and seventeen Hurricanes and six Fulmars intercepted the ninety-one B5Ns before the thirty-eight A6Ms could interfere. In the resulting combats, the British fighters claimed to have destroyed fifteen and damaged twenty-two of the enemy aircraft, for the loss of eight Hurricanes and a Fulmar. The actual score was two 'Kates' and one 'Zero' shot down and ten 'Kates' badly damaged; two more fighters were shot down by AA fire while strafing China Bay airfield.

The Japanese dive-bombers had taken no part in the raid as they were being held in reserve for a strike on the British Fleet. Instead, they were used to sink the small carrier *Hermes*, found in coastal waters south of Trincomalee. The D3As also sank four other ships in the area, but not until these smaller ships were under attack did eight Fulmars of 806 Squadron arrive from a shore airfield. The ships were not saved, but four 'Vals' were shot down and two damaged before some of their companions turned on the only marginally faster fighters and destroyed two.

The D3As shared in a second successful engagement as they returned to their carriers. Nine Bristol Blenheim light bombers of No 11 Squadron RAF became the first Allied aircraft to attack the Japanese carriers, approaching under cloud cover and near-missing *Akagi* in a level-bombing run at 12,000 feet. As they retired, the Blenheims were pursued by A6Ms and D3As which destroyed five and badly damaged the four surviving bombers. Two A6Ms were shot down by the bombers' gunners.

The Ceylon strikes cost the Japanese nineteen aircraft shot down and twenty-eight damaged. Only four A6Ms had been destroyed in air combat, whereas British losses totalled forty-three, eight of which were the victims of D3As. This was the British forces' only encounter with carrier-based enemy aircraft throughout the war and it bred a healthy respect for the efficiency of the Imperial Japanese Navy.

The Battle of the Coral Sea – May 1942 As the Japanese carrier force returned towards its home base, *Shokaku* and *Zuikaku* were detached to support the Army campaign in New Guinea. At the beginning of May, an amphibious landing force was about to sail for an assault on the south coast of New Guinea, with the object of capturing Port Moresby. The light carrier *Shoho* was already in the area, and would provide close cover, but in March *Lexington* and *Yorktown* had operated in the Coral Sea, between the island chain and Australia, and the Japanese needed the large carriers to deal with them.

In terms of numbers, the two American carriers had an edge over *Shokaku* and *Zuikaku*. Both sides had forty-two fighters, there were forty-two B5Ns to set against only twenty-five Douglas TBD-1 Devastators, but the US Navy was quantitively as well as qualitatively superior in its dive-bomber force, with seventy-four SBDs compared with only forty-one D3As. Neither of the Japanese carriers possessed radar, whereas both their opponents were so equipped, and *Yorktown* even had the much-needed IFF terminal equipment, although not all of her fighters were fitted with the aircraft set.

The Japanese carriers were technically inferior, but in tactics they were ahead of the Americans. At this time, and for some months to follow, the US Navy operated its carriers as singletons, with one Admiral in each carrier acting as the nucleus of a separate 'Task Force'. Complete freedom of action was given to the Task Force Commander to manoeuvre as he saw fit, within the requirements of the operation in hand. Japanese and British doctrine was to operate the carriers in a single formation, to benefit from the maximum anti-submarine and AA cover of a large screen. Fighter patrols were more easily co-ordinated and controlled by a single agency and the concentration meant that fewer fighters were needed to defend one large group than would be needed for several small separated groups. Five heavy cruisers and twelve destroyers had to be divided to provide screens for *Lexington* and *Saratoga*, and each carrier had to provide fighters for separate patrols and strike escort – not even the strikes were co-ordinated, although the simultaneous arrival of aircraft would have at least doubled the enemy's defensive problems.

Lexington and *Yorktown* moved into the Coral Sea at the beginning of May, as the Japanese forces were leaving Truk and Rabaul. On 4th May, *Yorktown*'s aircraft struck at Tulagi Island, where the Japanese had just established a base. The major success of the day, as far as the forthcoming battle was concerned, was the destruction of five H6K flying-boats – a considerable reduction in the enemy's force of shadowers. The first H6K to sight the American carriers was shot down by VF-42 on 5th May, when the two task forces came together again.

Zuikaku and *Shokaku* entered the Coral Sea on 6th May, passing between the Solomon Islands and the New Hebrides group. At noon, an undetected H6K sighted and reported the position of *Yorktown* and *Lexington* but the report was not forwarded to the Japanese carrier commander for 18 hours and the two forces passed within 80 miles of each other in poor weather at dusk on 6th May. *Shoho*, operating further to the north in support of the invasion convoy, was sighted by USAAF Boeing B-17s during the day and the American carriers closed in to strike her on 7th.

Shoho was sunk by *Yorktown's* aircraft before noon. Her few A6Ms failed to intercept the dive and torpedo-bombers, of which only three were lost. Meanwhile, *Shokaku* and *Zuikaku* had been fully misemployed, launching sixty sorties to sink an oiler and a destroyer which had been incorrectly identified as a carrier and a cruiser. Realising their mistake, the Japanese launched a search and strike mission of twelve D3As and fifteen B5Ns without fighter escort, to hunt for the American force. The latter had run into bad weather after sinking *Shoho* and were relying upon land-based searches to locate the enemy. Shortly before dusk, the Japanese strike was detected, returning to its carriers on a track well clear of *Lexington* and *Yorktown*. The VF-3 CAP was vectored out and intercepted the enemy above the cloud; nine aircraft were shot down, but the 'Vals' fought back and shot down two F4Fs which tried to dog-fight with them. The surviving D3As and B5Ns were split up and experienced considerable difficulty in finding their carriers – two groups attempted to join *Yorktown's* landing circuit and one was shot down by AA. Eleven bombers became operational losses, bringing the total to twenty-one out of the twenty-seven which had taken off.

The opposing forces located one another at about 0800 on 8th May and the strikes were delivered at around 1100. The two American carriers flew off sixty-nine attack aircraft and fifteen escorting F4Fs, but the two groups proceeded independently, 20 minutes apart. The Japanese strike, of fifty-one bombers and eighteen fighters, operated as a single unit to make a co-ordinated attack.

Yorktown's thirty-nine bombers and six fighters were not seen by the Japanese until the attack was well developed, thanks to the low cloud and rain which had made the carriers difficult to locate. The Dauntlesses scored two bomb hits on *Shokaku* but the Devastators failed to obtain a torpedo hit; the dozen A6Ms airborne failed to intercept the strike, which escaped without loss. *Lexington's* strike failed to locate the enemy in the expected position and only four Dauntlesses, the twelve Devastators and six F4Fs had sufficient fuel for a further search. The enemy carriers were soon sighted, but when the strike was still 15 miles distant the now-alert A6Ms intercepted, driving off the F4Fs but failing to stop the torpedo-bombers from attacking *Shokaku*. Further hits were claimed but none obtained, and five of the sixteen bombers were shot down, but only one F4F was destroyed.

While this unsuccessful attack was being delivered, the Japanese strike was occupying the American carriers. The raid was detected at 68 miles by *Lexington*, responsible for overall fighter direction. Eight F4Fs were on CAP, but at 10,000 feet, they were sandwiched between the D3As, at 18,000 feet, and the B5Ns and A6Ms, at 6,000 feet, and the *Lexington* FDO failed to obtain an accurate height estimation. To make matters worse, the CAP was low on fuel and therefore in no state to be required to climb at full power or even to fly far out to meet the raid. But the FDO did not even vector the F4Fs to a prudent distance, so that only three fighters saw the enemy before the attack developed. Nine fighters which had been scrambled could not form up and climb out in time to intercept. A dozen Dauntlesses had been stationed three miles outside the screen at 2,000 feet to break up torpedo-bomber attacks – had the Japanese employed tactics similar to those of the US Navy VT squadrons, boring in at low level, this might have been a useful disposition, but as it was the B5Ns and their escort swept in above the SBDs, only levelling out inside the destroyer screen. As it was the 'Speedies' performed very well, catching two B5Ns before release and two more as they withdrew, as well as a D3A and two A6Ms, for the loss of four SBDs. The F4Fs had become entangled with the A6Ms and were of little assistance to the defence of the carriers, both of which were attacked and hit, *Lexington* by two torpedoes and two bombs, and *Yorktown* by one 551 lb bomb.

There was no further air fighting in the battle. *Shokaku* was severely damaged but reached home, *Lexington* was lost some hours after the battle due to a petrol vapour explosion and subsequent fire. Neither side had any reason to feel any confidence in its defensive procedures. The A6Ms had failed to break up either Devastator torpedo attack and had then allowed many American aircraft to escape through their appallingly bad gunnery. The US Navy CAP had been mishandled by *Lexington* and the poor choice of patrol height had given the F4Fs no chance when they were at last given a vector. Lack of practical training was blamed for the use of faulty doctrine: the Pacific Fleet was insistent on the need for radio silence in the forward areas – without radio the carriers could not practise controlled interceptions. With few carriers available, time for training in 'safe' rear areas could not be spared.

In spite of the A6Ms' obvious superiority in fighter-fighter combat, the US Navy pilots were confident that their F4Fs were better all-round fighters. All were now armoured and self-sealing tanks had been fitted, so that several F4Fs hit hard by A6M cannon shells had returned in spite of severe damage. Incendiary ammunition had been provided for the 0.50 in machine guns and hits on the unprotected Japanese aircraft had resulted in some startling conflagrations. The F4F's N2 reflector sight was criticised by many pilots – its single deflection ring represented a crossing speed of only 50 knots, which meant that in a quarter or 'high side' attack on a 200-knot target the pilot was given no accurate deflection information until he was within 30° of the target's heading.

The new F4F-4 had arrived in Hawaii just too late to be issued to *Lexington* or *Yorktown*. A US Navy variant of the Royal Navy's folding-wing Martlet II, it was heavier than the -3 so that maximum speed was reduced to 318 mph at 19,000 feet and 275 mph at sea level, while the rate of climb at combat power fell from 2,700 feet per minute to just over 2,300 fpm. Feelings about the two extra guns were mixed – more experienced pilots believed that four guns with 400 rounds each were quite sufficient and that two more guns did not improve the likelihood of hits, while the reduced ammunition capacity of 240 rounds per gun gave too short a total firing time for prolonged combat. By the end of May, all three of the operational fighter squadrons – VF-3, VF-6 and VF-8 – had been armed with twenty-seven F4Fs apiece, the extra pilots coming from VF-42 and newly-trained replacements.

The Battle of Midway – June 1942 At the end of May 1942, seven Japanese carriers sailed in three separate, although co-ordinated, groups for a major operation, the main objective of which was to be the capture

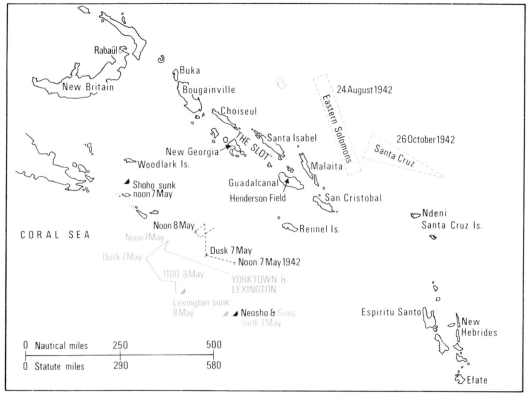

The Solomons Area.

of Midway Island, 1,300 statute miles to the north-west of Oahu. As a diversion, *Ryujo* and the new *Junyo* were to strike at the Aleutian Islands and cover the occupation of Attu and Kiska Islands. *Zuiho* was included in a central covering force which could go to the aid of the Aleutians force or the main Midway force, which was supported directly by *Akagi*, *Kaga*, *Hiryu* and *Soryu*. The latter were carrying an additional twenty-one A6Ms of the 6th Air Group, formed to provide fighters for *Junyo* and *Hiyo*; as the latter ship was not ready her fighters were loaned to the large carriers, bringing their fighter complement to 103 A6M2s.

Japanese intentions for Midway were known to the Americans, who had broken the enemy's cipher months earlier. Only three carriers were available, however, *Hornet* and *Enterprise*, both of which had taken part in the 'Tokyo Raid' in April, and *Yorktown*, undergoing hasty repairs at Pearl Harbour. *Hornet's* Air Group had had virtually no combat experience, *Enterprise* only a little more, but *Yorktown* embarked an improvised Air Group which was a mixture of her own and the lost *Lexington's*. The base air force on Midway had been reinforced and possessed over eighty fighters, bombers and reconnaissance aircraft. When, on 4th June 1942, the four Japanese carriers launched seventy-two strike aircraft and thirty-six fighters in a dawn strike against Midway, the three American carriers were only 250 miles to the east, and all twenty-eight Midway-based US Marine Corps fighters were airborne.

Directed by radar, the twenty-one F2A-3s and seven F4F-3s intercepted the B5Ns and D3As and destroyed four aircraft and damaged half-a-dozen others before the escort intervened. Two A6Ms were shot down thereafter, but thirteen F2As and three F4Fs were lost and seven others damaged beyond repair. AA fire destroyed three more Japanese aircraft, but the results of the battle were discouraging for the defenders, who had only five fighters left after the first round.

Midway's attack aircraft had taken off before dawn and fifty-three Martin B-26s, Grumman TBFs, Boeing B-17s, Vought SB2U Vindicators, and Dauntlesses attacked the carrier force in five unco-ordinated waves between 0710 and 0830. Seventeen A6Ms were on patrol between 3,000 and 20,000 feet when the B-26 and TBF torpedo-bombers were sighted at 14 miles; more fighters were scrambled, but again the 'Zeroes' failed to prevent the torpedoes from being launched and the American losses – seven aircraft out of ten destroyed and the other three badly damaged – were sustained at release and during withdrawal. Forty minutes after this attack, sixteen USMC Dauntlesses lost half their number, without scoring a hit. By now, thirty-six 'Zeroes' were airborne, in eleven sections, and two of these made a half-hearted attempt to attack sixteen B-17s, which made an unsuccessful level bombing run at 20,000 feet. The final wave – the eleven Vindicators – was prevented from attacking the carriers by the fighters, many of which were now making dummy attacks, their ammuni-

F4F-4 Wildcats of VF-8 test guns at *Hornet's* deck edge, framed by B-25 Mitchells of the 17th Bombardment Group USAAF, while en route to launch the latter for the April 25th Tokyo raid. (*USN*)

tion exhausted in earlier combats. Only two 'Wind Indicators' were lost, bringing the total to seventeen American strike aircraft destroyed, in addition to twelve damaged. Four A6Ms had been shot down by the bombers.

The Japanese fighters were unable to drive off the US Navy PBY-5 Catalina shadowers which used cloud cover to avoid interception throughout the day. The information from the shadowers was used to brief strikes launched in the usual unco-ordinated fashion from *Hornet* and *Enterprise* at 0700 and from *Yorktown* at 0840. The formations flew separately, on separate radio frequencies, so that no co-operation between Air Groups was possible; even the fighters, dive-bombers and torpedo-bombers from each ship proceeded separately, intending to achieve co-ordination in the target area!

Hornet's fighters and dive-bombers failed to find the enemy and proceeded to Midway – all ten VF-8 F4Fs ditched out of fuel short of the island. VF-6's ten fighters sighted the enemy first, at 0910, but the leader was loth to break radio silence and VB-6 and VS-6 were left to search for 40 minutes after they failed to find the enemy in the expected position. The first attack was delivered from 0930 by the Devastators of VT-8, which lacked the fuel to wait for fighter support. The fifteen torpedo-bombers were sighted by the Japanese at a distance of 20 miles and most of the twenty-four 'Zeroes' airborne descended upon them. VF-6, 6,000 feet above the massacre, watched but did nothing to help as the leader was waiting for a radio call for help which was being made on a different frequency. All of the TBDs were shot down and forty-four of the forty-five aircrew died; some did reach dropping positions, but the Japanese ships were well handled and evaded the slow American torpedoes. At least two A6Ms were shot down by TBD gunners.

Enterprise's VT-6 arrived 20 minutes after VT-8 and, without support from VF-6, which had left the area, suffered a similar fate to *Hornet's* TBDs, losing ten out of fourteen aircraft while near-missing *Hiryu* and *Soryu*. Even as the A6Ms were chasing the survivors of VT-6, *Yorktown's* VT-5 began the slow low-level approach, escorted by six F4Fs of VF-5. The attention of the defences had been distracted by VT-6, and not until VT-5 was crossing the outer screen of destroyers, three miles from the carriers, did a burst of AA fire attract the attention of the fighters. Nearly forty 'Zeroes' were now airborne, most at low level, and these concentrated on the eighteen American aircraft. *Hiryu's* nine fighters took on VF-5 and immediately destroyed one Wildcat and drove two others away severely damaged; Lieutenant Commander J. S. Thach and his two wingmen were unable to go assist the TBDs, but in their fight for survival they occupied a proportion of the defenders and remained unharmed. Five TBDs released torpedoes, two of which passed within 50 yards of *Kaga*, but only two aircraft escaped.

The A6Ms, assisted by AA fire, had destroyed thirty-six aircraft in less than 30 minutes, but had allowed the torpedo-bombers to reach attacking positions; had the US Navy possessed a torpedo as effective as those of the other warring nations, the Devastators might well have been rewarded for their sacrifice. All but seventeen A6Ms, all of which were below 5,000 feet, landed after VT-5's attack, but within a few minutes the Japanese

The only Devastator squadron in the Pacific Fleet which did not see action at the Coral Sea or destruction at Midway was *Saratoga*'s VT-3. By the time that the carrier completed repairs, the torpedo squadron had been re-armed with Grumman TBF Avengers. (*USN*) Left.
Almost as successful in air combat as the Wildcat was the SBD Dauntless. Here, a VB-6 Dauntless returns safely to *Enterprise*, in spite of extensive battle damage sustained while attacking the enemy carriers at Midway. (*USN*)

carriers were again having to scramble fighters, as dive-bombers had been sighted 22 miles away. These were VB-6 and VS-6 from *Enterprise* and VB-3 from *Yorktown*; the latter had flown straight to the correct position, whereas the former had searched for 40 minutes before sighting the enemy carriers. The A6Ms were unable to gain height in time to catch the dive-bombers before they were well established in their dives, and the SBDs pressed the attack home to inflict fatal damage on *Akagi*, *Kaga*, and *Soryu*. *Hiryu*, hidden by cloud, was not attacked. The Dauntlesses were hastened in their retreat by the A6Ms, but only seven out of fifty-four were

Used in very small numbers from the summer of 1942, the reconnaissance D4Y1-C 'Judy' was mistaken for the Messerschmitt Bf 109 by American fighter pilots who saw them at Midway and Santa Cruz.

claimed by the Japanese. Eleven of the others, all from *Enterprise*, ditched after running out of fuel on the return flight to their carrier.

At least eight A6Ms had been shot down during the *Enterprise* and *Yorktown* Air Groups' attacks, but twenty-three from the damaged carriers diverted to *Hiryu* at the end of their patrols. The one Japanese carrier now possessed her eighteen D3As, which had not yet been in action, nine serviceable B5Ns of her own and one of *Akagi's* and about forty A6Ms, as well as a Yokosuka D4Y-1C 'Judy' reconnaissance aircraft from *Soryu*. This aircraft had been on the initial dawn search mission which had failed to find the American carriers in time for the Japanese carriers to launch a strike before they were damaged. Once the search aircraft did locate the Americans the Aichi E13A 'Jake' floatplanes and the D4Y hung on relentlessly, reporting the carriers' movements without interference from fighters. Acting on their reports, *Hiryu* launched all of her D3As and six A6Ms at about 1100. The dive-bombers were armed with a 'mix' of twelve 551-lb anti-ship bombs and six 551-lb 'Land' bombs; at the time of the American attacks, the Japanese command had been undecided whether to strike at the American carriers or Midway, and the D3As' mixed load reflected an immediate decision taken aboard *Hiryu*.

Yorktown detected the strike at noon, when it was 46 miles to the west. The last of her own attack aircraft were returning at the same time, but the enemy were correctly identified and the twelve VF-5 Wildcats on CAP were vectored out in two groups, both at 10,000 feet. Successful interceptions were carried out at 20 and 15 miles, ten of the fighters making contact and destroying seven D3As and four A6Ms in a dog-fight. Seven or eight of the D3As did not jettison their bombs, but broke out of the mêlée to attack *Yorktown*. Six dive-bombers were shot down but three direct hits were scored, causing damage which brought the ship to a standstill. The *Enterprise* and *Hornet* CAPs took no part in the action, although their

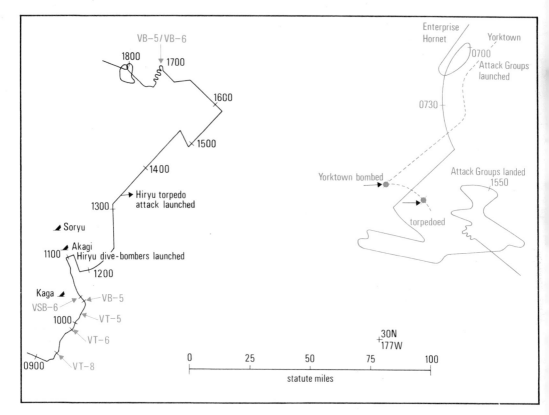

The Battle of Midway.

ships were only 20 miles away and the contribution of another dozen fighters might have been decisive. Two heavy cruisers and two destroyers were detached to reinforce *Yorktown's* screen, but the other carriers made no attempt to remain in the vicinity while *Yorktown* lay dead in the water for over an hour. The VF-5 fighters which had defended their ship refuelled and rearmed aboard *Enterprise*, and six of *Hornet's* fighters provided a CAP until they could return.

Hiryu launched the ten B5Ns at 1330, escorted by four of her own fighters and two *Kaga* survivors. The shadowers had continued to watch *Yorktown*, instead of the undamaged carriers and the Japanese strike headed for her. The heavy cruiser *Pensacola* was acting as radar guardship, for although the carrier was under way again and preparing to launch aircraft her CXAM had been destroyed. *Pensacola* detected the strike at 33 miles, and the six F4Fs on CAP were immediately sent out, four at 10,000 feet and two at 6,000 feet. Eight more Wildcats which had been refuelling were scrambled, but only four were clear of the ship before the enemy came within gun range.

The high CAP division failed to see the enemy, but the low pair were at the same height as the B5Ns and made contact at 12 miles. Only two B5Ns were shot down before the enemy split into two groups and attacked *York-town* from two sectors. The CAP and the fighters which had just taken off

A VF-5 Wildcat takes off during the Battle of Midway, watched by a sailor manning a 0.30 in AA machine gun on *Yorktown's* fo'csle. (*USN*)

chased the torpedo-bombers through the AA fire, and only four torpedoes were seen to be launched, two of which scored hits. Three more B5Ns and three A6Ms were shot down, as were four F4Fs. Only five B5Ns escaped – one of them *Akagi's* sole survivor, which took its torpedo home with it. *Hiryu* was now reduced to ten serviceable attack aircraft, about twenty-five A6Ms, and the single D4Y.

Yorktown had been severely damaged and she was abandoned prematurely ten minutes after she had been torpedoed. She did not actually sink until the early hours of 7th June, and then only after she had been torpedoed again, by a submarine. Her fighters and the SBDs of VS-5, which had located *Hiryu* at the time that their own carrier was undergoing attack, were recovered by *Enterprise*.

Enterprise launched twenty-four SBDs of VS-6 and VB-3 (ex-*Yorktown*) to attack *Hiryu* and these aircraft pushed over from 12,000 feet at 1700, undetected by the Japanese until the sun was reflected off their wings in the manoeuvre. One of the thirteen A6Ms on patrol managed to shoot down a VS-6 SBD in the dive and two others were shot down after bomb release, but the remainder escaped, having scored four fatal hits on *Hiryu*. An hour later, the A6Ms made their last interception: twelve B-17s missed the blazing carrier from medium level and were half-heartedly attacked by fighters which had little else to do but wait for their fuel to run out. The 'Zeroes' at last ditched around the force, all the pilots being picked up.

Although the Battle of Midway did not end until 7th June, when *Enter-*

Armourers begin re-arming VF-6's F4Fs even before the pilots are out of the cockpits – two aircraft at left 'F-18' and the aircraft behind are F4F-3As, without the supercharger 'lip' intake. The congestion caused on *Enterprise*'s deck by the lack of wing-folding capability is evident.

The most important shipboard reconnaissance aircraft used by the Japanese during the first year of the war was the Aichi E13A 'Jake' floatplane, carried by battleships and cruisers. (*via M. Passingham*)

prise and *Hornet* broke off the pursuit, the four Japanese carriers had all gone down by the early morning of 5th. The Japanese concentrated the three smaller carriers, but their contingency plans had not envisaged the loss of all four large carriers and they realised that a second carrier battle could result in an even more thorough reverse. *Ryujo* and *Junyo* had achieved little off the Aleutians and had suffered a few losses, while *Zuiho* had not been in action since January. Even with their reduced strength, the two American carriers were still more powerful and effective.

By any standards but those of naval air warfare, in which the protection of the ships was the final object, the Japanese fighters had scored an impressive victory. Of 195 American aircraft which had tried to attack the carriers, no fewer than sixty-five had been shot down and twenty F4Fs and F2As had been destroyed by strike escorts. But the A6Ms had not been able to stop the aptly-named Dauntlesses from *Yorktown* and *Enterprise*, which had turned Midway into an overwhelming victory for the US Navy.

The main cause of the Japanese defeat was their lack of a detection aid and of a satisfactory fighter direction system. Some remarkable sighting ranges were obtained – *Akagi's* look-outs saw one strike at 25 miles – but once the A6Ms joined in the defences tended to watch the fighting and the all-round watch was not maintained. On the other hand, the loss of *Yorktown* was due to doctrinal shortcomings. By operating as a single unit, she was left with only her own fighters to defend her. At the time of the second attack, *Enterprise* and *Hornet* were 40 miles away and only six F4Fs were on CAP. VF-6 and VF-8 made no practical contribution on 5th June and their thirteen losses were all through fuel exhaustion. Thach's VF-5 lost five F4Fs in combat and five others by accident, but they destroyed twenty-five Japanese aircraft, including seven A6Ms, sharing some of the D3As and B5Ns with *Yorktown* and her screen's AA gunners.

As a yardstick by which the day's air fighting may be gauged, seventy German and thirty British aircraft fell in combat on 15th August 1940 – statistically the RAF's most successful day of the Battle of Britain. At Midway, eighty-five American and fifty Japanese aircraft were destroyed in the air, all but a score as the result of fighter action.

Malta Convoys — Summer 1942

After the loss of *Ark Royal*, Force 'H' was without a large carrier which could be used for major operations until the old *Eagle* joined, in March 1942. Smaller than *Ark* and the armoured carriers, she could carry eighteen Swordfish and four Sea Hurricanes, the latter being attached to 813 Squadron. By means of a minor modification to the engine manifold pressure control, the maximum 'boost' was raised from $+6\frac{1}{2}$ lb (49 in Hg) to $+16$ lb (68 in Hg), so that the maximum speed at 7,500 feet was 315 mph – some 25 mph faster than the original RAF Hurricane at this height. The engine life was considerably reduced when such high boost was used, but as British engines of the period still used carburettors instead of direct injection or fuel metering systems, such additives as water/methanol or nitrous oxide could not be employed.

Force 'H' was not called upon to escort a convoy until June 1942, by

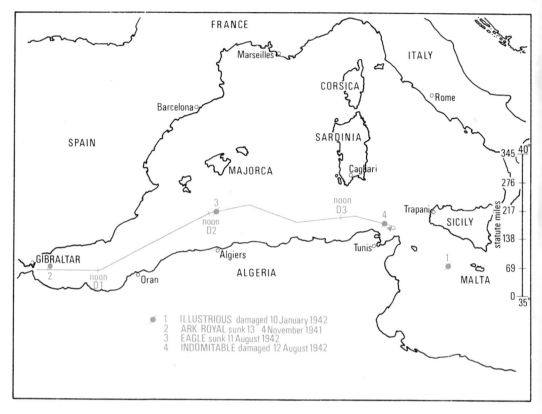

The Malta "Pedestal" Convoy.

Map labels:
FRANCE
Marseilles
CORSICA
ITALY
Rome
Barcelona
SARDINIA
SPAIN
Cagliari
MAJORCA
noon D3
Trapani
SICILY
3
noon D2
4
GIBRALTAR
Algiers
Tunis
2
noon D1
Oran
ALGERIA
MALTA

statute miles
345 40°
276
217
138
69
0
35°

1 ILLUSTRIOUS damaged 10 January 1942
2 ARK ROYAL sunk 13 4 November 1941
3 EAGLE sunk 11 August 1942
4 INDOMITABLE damaged 12 August 1942

Sea Hurricane
Aircraft flown by Sub Lieutenant P. J. Hutton of 801 Squadron – the only fighter
from *Eagle* to survive Operation 'Pedestal'.

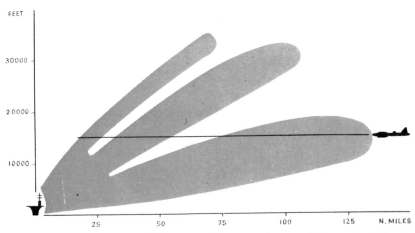

FEET

30000

20000

10000

25   50   75   100   125   N. MILES

Typical 1941–45 radar vertical coverage diagram: the gaps between the 'lobes' were in fact of assistance to the Fighter Direction Officer, for by plotting the ranges at which aircraft faded and re-appeared, the height of the target could be estimated with fair accuracy.

Opposite centre. When USS *Wasp* arrived at Scapa Flow to join the British Home Fleet, her Air Group disembarked to fly from the Royal Naval Air Station, Hatston. Maintenance crews of VF-7 and VT-7 line up in front of the F4F-4 and TBDs while an 809 Squadron Fulmar is manhandled on the apron. (*IWM A9439*)

which time Malta's situation had become desperate. The Luftwaffe had returned to Sicily at the beginning of the year and by May Malta's air and sea striking forces were no longer capable of effective action and the island itself was in danger of invasion. Over 200 Spitfires were flown from *Eagle* and USS *Wasp* between March and June 1942, in eight operations, but once on Malta their losses were very high and they were unable to achieve air superiority. Fuel, ammunition, and food were all running short by mid-1942, and a convoy was necessary. In fact, two convoys were run simultaneously, one from Egypt and one from Gibraltar. The western operation would have the benefit of Force 'H's carrier, but although it had been intended that the eastern should be accompanied by the Royal Navy's first American-built escort carrier – *Archer* – which was to be armed with the ten Grumman Martlet IIIs (F4F-3As) of 805 Squadron, the carrier suffered a serious mechanical breakdown and the convoy had to depend upon land-based air cover.

Operation 'Harpoon' began on 12th June 1942, when six fast merchant ships sailed through the Straits of Gibraltar and were met by Force 'H'. *Eagle* was accompanied by the even older *Argus*, the former carrying the four Sea Hurricanes of 813 Squadron, twelve more of 801 Squadron and four Fulmars of 807 Squadron, based at Gibraltar since the loss of '*Ark*'. Five more 807 Squadron Fulmars were aboard *Argus*, together with half-a-dozen Swordfish. The intention was to maintain standing patrols of four Sea Hurricanes at high level and two Fulmars at low level during the crucial day spent to the south of Sardinia.

The convoy was shadowed almost continuously during the second day, but the only kill was scored by 813 Squadron, at dusk. Once the convoy had been detected, its progress could easily be predicted by the enemy, for it had to pass through the narrow channel between Sardinia and Algeria and there was little room for deceptive track alterations.

The Italian Air Force in Sardinia delivered a maximum effort attack between 1000 and 1200 on 14th June. The raid was to consist of co-ordina-

Few photographs survived the sinking of *Eagle*, and this poor quality shot is the only one known of an 813 Squadron Sea Hurricane, seen just after landing. (*A. J. Ward*)

Throughout 1941 and 1942, the most numerous shipping strike aircraft used by the Axis was the Savoia Marchetti SM.79 *aerosilurante*, this particular example belonging to the 281st Squadron, which took part in the June and August 1942 battles.

ted waves of fighter-bombers which were to attack the carriers immediately before torpedo and level bombers attacked the convoy. Half an hour before the eight Fiat CR.42AS fighter-bombers attacked, a formation of torpedo-bombers was detected 20 miles from the convoy, apparently awaiting the CR.42 overture. The SM.79s were dispersed by an 801 Squadron patrol, which shot one down and forced some of the others to jettison their torpedoes. When the CR.42s did attack, they concentrated only on *Argus*, missed her, and lost two of their number to that ship's Fulmars. Two other fighter-bombers were so hounded that they lacked the fuel to return to base and diverted to Algeria, where they were interned by the French.

The main attack did not come for another 40 minutes. It was the biggest Italian raid yet seen, and consisted of thirty-two SM.79 torpedo-bombers and eighteen SM.84 level bombers, escorted by thirty-nine Macchi MC.200 fighters. The six Sea Hurricanes and four Fulmars intercepted the torpedo-bombers at between 15 and 10 miles, but the escort overwhelmed them by sheer weight of numbers, so that only four bombers were shot down and at least twenty-eight SM.79s managed to release about forty torpedoes. A merchant ship was hit and sunk outright and a light cruiser was heavily damaged but managed to limp back to Gibraltar, absorbing the Sardinian air effort for the rest of the day. Three SM.79s had been shot down by AA fire, as had a Fulmar; another Fulmar had been shot down by the Macchis, which had lost three of *their* number to the carrier fighters.

Not until late afternoon did the convoy come under attack from Sicily. At 1820, ten Junkers Ju 88s were detected at over 50 miles at about 16,000 feet, and these were intercepted by Fulmars which destroyed two of the bombers and forced two others to jettison their bombs. The remainder broke away from the fighters and dived unseen by the convoy screen, which had been warned of the attack but whose vision was impaired by haze. All the bombs missed.

Two hours later, shortly before dusk, the Luftwaffe and Regia Aeronautica delivered a combined attack, by eleven Ju 88s, forty-six SM.79s and seventeen Ju 87s (flown by Italian crews), escorted by twenty-seven Messerschmitt Bf 109Fs and forty-three Macchi Mc.202s. Six Sea Hurricanes and two Fulmars were airborne to defend the convoy. The Ju 88s and thirty-two of the SM.79s made an attempt to draw off the fighters by making an ineffectual level attack from high level. The fourteen torpedo-bombers meanwhile worked around into a favourable sector for the attack, watched over by their escort and marked by the carrier fighters. This manoeuvring took 20 minutes, and in this 'lull', the seventeen 'Stukas' made an unprofitable premature attack on the destroyer screen, attempting to open a gap for the torpedo aircraft. When the latter did attack, they were intercepted by the Hurricanes, which shot down two SM.79s before the escort claimed their full attention, destroying a Hurricane. The convoy AA shot down another torpedo-bomber, as well as a Fulmar which had continued the pursuit into the gun defence zone. *Argus* and the battleship *Malaya* were both narrowly missed by torpedoes, some of which were released from as close as 400 yards.

The heavy escort turned back at dusk, leaving the convoy to make the next day's passage under the cover of Malta's Spitfires. An anti-aircraft

An 801 Squadron Sea Hurricane returns to *Eagle* during the 'Harpoon' convoy operation. The tail of another fighter can be seen to the right of the picture. (*P. J. Hutton*)

cruiser directed the fighters to several successful interceptions during 15th June, but land-based fighters unaccustomed to the needs of shipping defence could not be expected to function as effectively as carrier fighters and three more merchant ships were sunk by air attack before the convoy reached Malta. The eastern convoy had turned back on the previous day, unable to go on in the face of unrelenting air attack without fighter cover.

Force 'H' had looked after its charges remarkably well. The twenty-five fighters and the AA guns had fought off 142 bombers and 104 fighters, losing one merchant ship sunk and a cruiser damaged, as well as two Sea Hurricanes and two Fulmars to enemy action. Between 13th and 16th June, twenty-four Axis aircraft had been claimed – in fact, thirty were destroyed, sixteen by fighters, eleven by AA fire, and three indeterminable.

In spite of the 'victory', the Royal Navy was conscious that its fighters had serious shortcomings and that defensive techniques required improvement. The Fulmar was far too slow, both in level speed and climb, and it was no match for the Axis escort fighters; although the Hurricane was faster, its endurance of little more than an hour was too low for safety, direction officers and pilots being reluctant to attempt interceptions beyond 25 miles. But the main fault with both fighters was their totally inadequate armament. By August 1942, Britain was half-way through the war, and British-built naval fighters were still armed with 0.303 in Browning guns. RAF fighters had been armed with 20 mm Hispano and Oerlikon cannon since 1940, but in spite of successful trials with a Fulmar cannon installation, there were not sufficient guns to spare to permit the Navy to undertake a modification programme.

Operation 'Pedestal' – August 1942 The convoy run to Malta in August 1942 – Operation 'Pedestal' – has been given more coverage in print than any other convoy with the exception of PQ 17, which was cut to pieces in the Arctic in July 1942. The stores run in by 'Harpoon' would not meet the island's needs for long, and a bigger delivery was urgently needed. The object of 'Pedestal' was to run thirteen 14-knot merchant ships and a tanker – the famous *Ohio* – from Gibraltar to the Sicilian Narrows under cover of a powerful heavy escort; the 'heavies' would turn back at dusk on the third day, leaving four cruisers and a destroyer screen to protect the convoy during the night and the following day's passage. Air cover on 13th August would come from Malta-based Beaufighters and Spitfires, controlled by two of the cruisers.

Three carriers were included in the heavy escort, with a total of seventy-two fighters embarked. *Eagle's* squadrons had seen recent action, but of the six fighter squadrons aboard *Victorious* and *Indomitable* only two – 809 and 880 – had been embarked for more than three months with their current aircraft. 884 and 885 Squadrons had not been formed long, and only the latter had seen any combat, and while 800 and 806 had been in commission for some time they had been re-armed with Sea Hurricanes and Martlet IIs only at the end of June. *Victorious* had to maintain her five non-folding Sea Hurricanes on deck as her lifts were too small, and so her main role was to provide the low-level defence with the sixteen Fulmars, most of which were brand new and therefore possessed a better performance than the 1941 Fulmars or those of 807 Squadron. *Indomitable* had been built with an enlarged forward lift and with greater hangar area than her half-sister, and could stow most of her thirty-one fighters under cover. The Martlets were intended to patrol at medium level, with the Hurricanes above them at 20,000 feet. During the critical day's passage to the south of Sardinia eighteen fighters would be maintained on patrol at all times, with as many more at immediate readiness; if attack appeared to be imminent, then twelve more fighters would be flown off, so that a total of forty-eight fighters might be airborne at once.

Eagle	801 Squadron	12 Sea Hurricanes (plus four spare)
	813 Squadron	4 Sea Hurricanes
Victorious	809 Squadron	10 Fulmar IIs
	884 Squadron	6 Fulmar IIs
	885 Squadron	5 Sea Hurricanes
Indomitable	800 Squadron	12 Sea Hurricanes
	806 Squadron	9 Martlet IIs
	880 Squadron	10 Sea Hurricanes

This was air power on a huge scale by Royal Navy standards. The defensive doctrine had been worked out during the previous year, but the three carriers had never worked before, and so the Navy permitted itself a dress rehearsal to the west of Gibraltar, from 6th to 8th August. This proved to be of inestimable value to ships, FDOs, and pilots alike and several amendments were made to the existing orders in consequence. *Victorious's* Type 79B radar had better 'height finding' characteristics than *Indomitable's* Type 281, which had a better low-altitude capability, so that she and the similarly fitted *Sirius* (AA cruiser) would maintain an all-round search while *Victorious* and other cruisers concentrated on the vital height finding. Very High Frequency (VHF) R/T was fitted in the ships for the exchange of information, and all fighters were equipped with VHF and, of course, IFF.

Identification of aircraft was given considerable attention: to avoid repetition of the unfortunate loss of carrier fighters to 'friendly' AA fire,

entirely new joining instructions were issued. When approaching the convoy, fighters were to fly in a stepped-up line-astern formation, coming in from the opposite side to the sun. When five miles from the centre of the convoy, the formation would make a complete orbit, to permit radar and visual 'de-lousing' to ensure that the fighters had not been followed home by undesirables, or even that they were not an enemy formation approaching in an unusual formation. Only when in hot pursuit of the enemy were the rules to be disregarded, and to protect the fighters from over-eager gunners the leading edges of the wings were painted yellow, as was the fin, to provide a high-visibility visual identification mark.

On 10th August, as the convoy entered the Mediterranean, the enemy air forces based on Sardinia and Sicily possessed ninety torpedo-bombers, ninety-four medium bombers, fifty-seven dive-bombers and fighter-bombers, and 247 fighters. Two U-boats and half-a-dozen Italian submarines lay across the narrow path of the convoy, to assist as shadowers and raiders.

The first report to reach the enemy came from Vichy French Algeria. Early on 11th August, *Indomitable's* Sea Hurricanes shepherded an Air France civil aircraft away from the convoy. On landing at Algiers, the crew informed the authorities, who in turn passed on the intelligence to the Italian Armistice Commission. Even without this curious behaviour on the part of a neutral the enemy would have located the ships during the forenoon, for the visibility was almost unlimited and there was no cloud. From 0815 it was obvious that shadowers were about, but instead of the usual Cant. Z.1007*bis* at low level, these were Ju 88s, at and above 20,000 feet. One of these was damaged during the forenoon, but not until mid-

10th August, 1942: An Albacore takes off from *Indomitable* for an anti-submarine patrol. In the foreground, aboard *Victorious*, two 885 Squadron Sea Hurricanes stand-by at immediate readiness for a scramble. (*IWM A15961*)

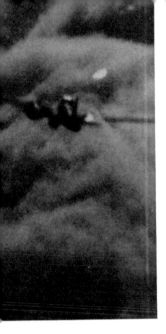

A Junkers Ju 88D of (F)/122, the Luftwaffe's Mediterranean long-range reconnaissance unit, dives for the clouds to escape naval fighters which have set its starboard engine on fire. (*D. G. Parker*)

Above right.
HMS *Indomitable* was recalled from the Indian Ocean to take part in the 'Pedestal' convoy operation. Here she is seen during a brief refuelling stop at Freetown, with Sea Hurricanes of 800 and 880 Squadrons and Martlets of 806 Squadron on deck, ahead of Fairey Albacore biplane torpedo-bombers. (*IWM A11167*)

afternoʊ. did the Commanding Officer of 880 Squadron, Lieutenant Commander F. E. C. Judd, score the first kill of 'Pedestal', sending a Ju 88 down in flames from 19,000 feet. One Sea Hurricane was hit by return fire and had to ditch alongside a destroyer.

In the meantime, the first serious loss had been experienced. *Eagle* was torpedoed and sunk by U-73 at 1300, when some 60 miles north of Algiers. Four of her 801 Squadron aircraft were on patrol and landed aboard the other carriers, but sixteen Hurricanes were lost. This was a serious blow, coming before the battle was joined, and the strength of the stand-by force and the patrols was cut by eight Sea Hurricanes immediately.

As dusk was approaching, a raid was detected at 50 miles. Only four 880 Squadron fighters were on patrol at the time, stalking a Ju 88 shadower which they later damaged, and the two carriers flew off another fifteen Sea Hurricanes and four Fulmars. The decision to commit so many fighters was of doubtful wisdom, for in the gathering darkness the crews had great difficulty in seeing the raiders and the FDOs were unable to give assistance as the radar screen and plots were so cluttered, while the ships equipped with blind-fire radar control for their AA guns were severely hampered. In the mêlée which followed, an 880 pilot damaged a Ju 88, 809 Squadron drove off two more, and ships' AA destroyed four more – out of a total force of nine. The few He 111 torpedo-bombers remained well clear of the convoy, which suffered no damage.

The recovery which followed was chaotic. Visibility had fallen to 500 yards, and fighters approaching the carriers were fired on by AA. Three Fulmars landed 'on the first ship which didn't fire at us' and found themselves on board *Indomitable*; one collided with a gun mounting and had to be thrown over the side to clear the deck. Three Sea Hurricanes of 885 also landed aboard 'Indom', but without mishap. Not so the 880 Squadron Hurricane which went to *Victorious* – landing against a 'wave-off', it damaged an 885 aircraft on a deck-edge outrigger and was itself burned out

after hitting the safety barrier. An 885 Squadron Sea Hurricane damaged another out-rigged aircraft, and a third, of 801, was hit by the only Fulmar to return to *Victorious*. Three fighters were thus written off and four damaged; the losses for the day totalled four in accidents, one in combat, and sixteen with *Eagle*. No pilots had been lost, but only fifty-one fighters remained.

August 12th, 1942, was a significant day in the history of air warfare. The Luftwaffe and Regia Aeronautica delivered three raids, by nearly 200 attack aircraft of all types, escorted by over 100 fighters, but at the time that the heavy escort turned back in the evening, no merchant ship had been sunk, although one had been hit by a bomb, one destroyer had been sunk by torpedo, and *Indomitable* had been bombed and put out of action (as a carrier). At no time did the number of naval fighters airborne exceed twenty-four, six to eight of which were Fulmars.

The first raid was detected at 0900, at a range of 65 miles, and consisted of nineteen Ju 88s from Sicily, escorted by sixteen Bf 109s. Eight Sea Hurricanes of 800 and 880 Squadrons were on patrol at 20,000 feet, as well as a pair of 884 Squadron Fulmars at low level, and another eleven Sea Hurricanes and four Fulmars were scrambled. The two fighter divisions already airborne intercepted the raid at 25 miles, destroying four Ju 88s and damaging four others which dropped out of the formation. The Bf 109 escort failed to catch the interceptors before the Ju 88s pushed over into shallow glide attacks, and even thereafter they were able to destroy only one 880 Squadron aircraft. The bombers were met by the fighters which had just taken off and more were shot down, damaged and turned away, so that only four reached the convoy to miss the ships. An 801 Squadron Sea Hurricane was shot down and three other fighters damaged in the low level pursuit. Nine Ju 88s had been destroyed and six were claimed as damaged.

809 and 884 Squadrons picked off shadowers throughout the day, but

Eagle launches her last fighter patrol – noon, 11th August, 1942. An hour later she was torpedoed and sunk by *U-73*. (*IWM A11157*)

the Z.1007*bis* were available in sufficient numbers to enable a continuous watch to be maintained at low level, while Ju 88s shadowed uninterrupted from above 30,000 feet.

The second major raid was detected shortly before noon, when the convoy was 70 miles south of Sardinia. Enemy formations were plotted as they moved to the east to begin their approach. When the ninety-eight attack aircraft and their forty escorting fighters began to close in, there were four Martlets and four Sea Hurricanes at 20,000 feet, and two Fulmars at 10,000 feet over the convoy. These were immediately reinforced by six Sea Hurricanes and four Fulmars. In spite of the imminence of air attack, *Indomitable* continued to refuel and re-arm fighters on deck.

To open the attack, the Italians had provided a group of ten SM.84s armed with long-range circling torpedoes (Motobomba FF), to be dropped in the path of the convoy in order to force the ships to break up the formidable defensive screen by taking evasive action. The SM.84s were assisted by eight CR.42 fighter-bombers which would attack the screen to open a gap for forty-three SM.79 and SM.84 torpedo-bombers which would take advantage of the disorganisation. Thirty-seven Ju 88s would deliver a shallow diving attack as the torpedo-bombers ran in. Special attacks consisted of two Reggiane Re.2001 fighter-bombers, which were to drop anti-personnel fragmentation bombs on the carriers' decks, and a radio-controlled SM.79, packed with explosive, which would be guided on to a suitable large target.

The co-ordination needed for the attack was not achieved. The first eighteen Ju 88s lost one of their number to the Martlets, the SM.84s carrying circling torpedoes were intercepted at 40 miles by Fulmars and were subsequently harried by the other fighters, and the CR.42s attacked only one destroyer – which they missed. The escort fighters tied up some of the carrier aircraft, but sufficient managed to break away from the Mc.202s to demoralise the two groups of SM.79 torpedo-bombers as they made their approach. At least a dozen were shot down or forced to jettison their torpedoes, and those which continued on to release against the ships did so from outside the screen, so that no hits were obtained, although many were claimed. The last major wave of this attack consisted of the other nineteen Ju 88s. These were intercepted by 809 Squadron's Fulmars at 19,000 feet and several were damaged and forced to jettison their bombs. The Fulmars were unable to keep up with the bombers when the latter started their dive, and the one damaging hit of the raid was scored by a Ju 88, which bombed the freighter *Deucalion*, which was obliged to drop out of the convoy, although she was not sunk until the evening.

The special attack came to nothing. The Re.2001s were mistaken for Sea Hurricanes and were not fired upon, but one missed *Victorious*, while a bomb from the other bounced off the armoured deck and broke up. The guided-bomb SM.79 went out of control and crashed in Algeria – much to the wrath of the Vichy French authorities.

Apart from the presence of shadowers, the convoy passed a quiet afternoon, and not until 1700 was there any sign of further attack. As in the case of the noon attack, over an hour's warning was given, thanks to the enemy forming up within radar range. The raid was smaller than the earlier effort, consisting of fourteen SM.79s, twenty-nine Ju 87s (seventeen flown by

Italian crews, and eighteen Ju 88s, covered by about forty fighters. The first sighting was made by a Martlet patrol, which was vectored out to 30 miles: the enemy formation proved to be one of six bombers protected by twenty-plus fighters and the Martlets were ordered to return to the vicinity of the convoy. At about 1800, the enemy began to deploy to attack from two directions; eleven separate groups were tracked, at heights of between 10,000 and 25,000 feet, between 50 and 60 miles from the convoy. At this time, there were three Martlets, twelve Sea Hurricanes, and six Fulmars airborne. By 1830, when the enemy started to close in, *Victorious* was launching four Fulmars and two Hurricanes and *Indomitable* was preparing to catapult four more Hurricanes. The heavy covering force turned to the west shortly before the attack, which ignored the convoy entirely.

Only eight fighters were sent out to intercept the enemy groups approaching from the south-east and north-east, the remainder being held in reserve to fight a close-in battle. All were engaged by Bf 109s and Mc.202s and on this occasion the escort was far more determined, so that relatively few of the interceptors could get at the bombers. As *Indomitable* was completing her last launch, she was attacked and hit by the twelve Luftwaffe Stukas, which scored two hits and put the carrier out of action. The Sea Hurricane division which had just taken off destroyed five of the Ju 87s after the attack, and apart from one SM.79, these were the only bombers to fall to the carrier fighters in this attack. The SM.79s scored their only success of the operation by torpedoing the destroyer *Foresight*, which sank while in tow on the following day.

Victorious recovered the fighters at the end of the attack, leaving only seven Fulmars and two Sea Hurricanes to cover the convoy. The last patrol of the day landed at 2040. After jettisoning a number of damaged aircraft

'Stukas' were used by the Italian *Regia Aeronautica* as well as the Luftwaffe for attacks on the Malta convoys, and on 12th August Ju 87s scored their third success against a British carrier, damaging *Indomitable* during the last raid of the day.

After 'Pedestal' many Royal Navy fighter squadrons were re-armed with the Supermarine Seafire, the 'navalised' deck-landing variant of the RAF's Spitfire. The first victory scored by the type occurred on 8th November, 1942, during the North African landings, when two 885 Squadron pilots from HMS *Formidable* (pictured) destroyed a Vichy DB-7 (Douglas A-20). (*IWM A.14167 and D. R. Whittaker*)

to make room for those which were less unserviceable, *Victorious* had eight Sea Hurricanes, three Martlets, and ten Fulmars – exactly the same number as she had possessed on passing Gibraltar. Seven fighters had been lost in combat during the day – three Fulmars, three Sea Hurricanes, and a Martlet, but when the claims were analysed the pilots were credited with thirty-eight victories, four by the Martlets, nine by the outclassed Fulmars, and twenty-five by the Sea Hurricanes. Four pilots and two Fulmar telegraphists were lost with their aircraft.

By any standards, the shipboard fighters had scored a victory. The enemy had held the initiative throughout 12th August, attacking in great strength, with an escort which always outnumbered the defenders. Not until the third raid did the fighters manage to subdue the tired naval pilots, most of whom were flying their third or fourth sorties of the day. Even then, the sixty-one attack aircraft managed to obtain only two really damaging hits and they neglected the convoy, which was of far greater strategic significance.

The convoy did get through, but only just. During the night of 12th/13th August and throughout the day of 14th, Axis torpedo boats, submarines, and aircraft sank eight more ships and damaged the two fighter-direction cruisers (one later sank). Four freighters and the tanker *Ohio* reached Malta, all damaged. The stores they brought were sufficient to save the island and keep it going until November, when the last relief convoy arrived and marked the end of the siege of Malta.

Five great convoys had been run through the Mediterranean between May 1941 and August 1942. Forty freighters, troopships and transports had been protected by aircraft from *Ark Royal*, *Formidable*, *Eagle*, *Argus*, *Victorious* and *Indomitable*, but only two had been hit by enemy aircraft while a carrier was with the convoy (*Tanimbar* in June 1942, *Deucalion* in August 1942). Over 400 German and Italian aircraft had closed the convoys, to shadow or attack, and they had experienced over 25 per cent losses – eight-six shot down by fighters and at least thirty-five by AA fire.

The fighters used by the Royal Navy were outdated by the standards of the European War, but the formulation and continuous revision of tactics gave the squadrons a decided advantage over the enemy bombers, and the *élan* displayed in defence had a serious effect on the morale of Axis aircrew. The Royal Navy laid down the ground rules for carrier task force operation during the Mediterranean operations, and 'Pedestal' was to prove to be the British carrier pilots' 'finest hour'.

The conclusions and recommendations arising from Royal Navy experience were passed on to the US Navy without delay, and the latter service adopted many British procedures. In July 1943, *Victorious* operated in the South-West Pacific area with *Saratoga* – the British ship was unable to operate her Grumman TBF-1 Avengers with the same efficiency as the American carrier, but her fighter direction efficiency was superior, so that she exchanged her 832 Squadron for VF-3, to operate thirty-six Martlets and twenty-four F4F-4s as a defensive fighter carrier. 'Sara' retained twelve Wildcats to escort her seventy strike aircraft. Before the end of the year, however, the new carriers of the Essex and Independence classes were coming into service, with much improved fighter-direction arrangements. From that point, the US Navy led the way.

Opposite. Below right. Not what it appears to be! This aircraft is a Royal Navy Martlet II of 888 Squadron (*Formidable*), wearing US Navy markings adopted for all British naval aircraft during the invasion of Algeria. The 'Torch Star' was used to lessen the risk of any misidentification through confusion between the British and French tricolour roundels. (*D. R. Whittaker*)

The Pacific — 1942-43 — Marking Time

Guadalcanal Two months after the Battle of Midway, the US Marines invaded Tulagi and Guadalcanal. Three carriers – *Enterprise*, *Saratoga*, and *Wasp* – covered the landings on 7th August, which were completely successful. The ninety-nine F4F-4 Wildcats were used for ground attack missions as well as for defensive patrols over the beach-head and the carrier force. Six hours after the first Marines had landed, the first Japanese bomber attack arrived – twenty-seven 'Betties' from Rabaul, escorted by eighteen 'Zeroes' of the veteran Tainan Air Group. A coastwatcher on Bougainville Island gave an hour's warning, but the inexperience of the fighter-direction cruiser *Chicago*, controlling the fighters inshore, resulted in the CAP failing to intercept until the medium-level bombers were over the anchorage. The twenty Wildcats of VF-5 (*Saratoga*) and VF-6 (*Enterprise*) destroyed four bombers and a 'Zero', but the American fighters suffered heavily at the hands of the escort, which shot down nine Wildcats and damaged several others. Another A6M was shot down by a VB-6 Dauntless, but VS-72 (*Wasp*) lost a dive-bomber to the fighters.

An hour and a half later, sixteen 'Val' dive-bombers attacked without warning, damaged a destroyer, and were then cut to pieces by VF-5 and

VF-6, which claimed fourteen out of the sixteen, at no cost to themselves. It would appear that the Wildcats over-claimed, but the admitted loss of ten aircraft was a severe blow to the Japanese.

On 8th August, twenty 'Betty' torpedo-bombers attacked, escorted by twenty-four A6Ms. The approach was made at low level and no radar warning was obtained – the first sighting being made by a VF-6 CAP 17,000 feet above the target. The four F4Fs dived to intercept the raid and destroyed four G4Ms and an A6M. The survivors ran into the concentrated AA fire of the mass of shipping and another thirteen torpedo-bombers crashed. One torpedo hit was scored on a destroyer which became a total loss. As the three fortunate G4Ms withdrew, one was bounced and shot down by a VS-71 SBD. Sixty-three aircraft had attacked the Guadalcanal invasion shipping, and thirty-one had been lost to fighters and AA. The only return for the sacrifice was the destruction of one destroyer and the damaging of another, in addition to the eleven US Navy aircraft shot down.

The carriers withdrew from the Guadalcanal area on 8th August and proceeded to Noumea to replenish and make good their losses. The Marines on Guadalcanal and their supporting warships were thereby left without fighter cover until 20th August, when the escort carrier Long Island flew off nineteen F4F-4s of Marine Fighting Squadron (VMF-) 223 to Henderson Field. Task Force 61 – the American carrier force – meanwhile waited for the Japanese Fleet to react to the invasion.

By 16th August, the Japanese had managed to assemble a carrier force with a trained complement of aircrew. Shokaku, Zuikaku and Ryujo possessed seventy-four A6Ms, forty-one D3As, and fifty-two B5Ns between them; this concentration was, however, at the expense of the other carriers – Junyo, Zuiho and Hiyo, which had to set about forming up new groups around only a small experienced nucleus of pilots. One new feature was the radar fitted to Shokaku; with a range of only 40 miles, it was inferior to the Allied sets, and it was not tied in to a direction organisation, but it did at least give the Japanese some long-range warning capability.

The Eastern Solomons The three Japanese carriers headed for the Solomons with the dual task of supporting a reinforcement operation and seeking out the American carriers. The clash came on 24th August, in what was called the Battle of the Eastern Solomons.

It was probably the least flattering carrier battle of all, for neither side showed that it had profited from the lessons of Coral Sea and Midway and the defending fighters undoubtedly failed. The two big Japanese carriers were operating 90 miles away from Ryujo and although a succession of SBD and TBF search teams found and reported the enemy disposition, the undisciplined 'chatter' of the F4F CAP pilots on the same R/T frequency prevented several reports from getting through. The search aircraft attacked the Japanese carriers in pairs, but only one was shot down by an A6M, and another 'Zero' which attempted to intercept suffered the ignominy of being shot down by Japanese AA fire. A Saratoga strike, operating independently as usual, failed to find Shokaku and Zuikaku but sank Ryujo; no Japanese fighters intercepted this strike. In mid-afternoon, Enterprise and Saratoga began to launch simultaneous strikes. At the

A 'Zero' takes off from one of the smaller Japanese carriers during the late summer of 1942. (*USN 80-G-182252*)

time, search aircraft from both carriers were returning in small groups, *Saratoga's* strike was starting to return from the area of the sinking *Ryujo*, and twenty-nine bombers and twelve fighters were on their way from the other two Japanese carriers. The first warning of the enemy raid was a single large radar contact at 90 miles: this was sufficient to alert the American defences, and thirty-eight F4Fs were airborne by the time that contact was regained after a 17-minute interval. A VF-6 division sighted the enemy at 33 miles and attacked the nine B5Ns at 6,000 feet, breaking up the formation and claiming to have shot down three torpedo-bombers. From this time until the end of the attack, the endless chatter of the Wildcat pilots completely jammed the R/T, so that *Enterprise's* FDO could not control his fighters, increased to fifty-three by the time that the enemy had closed to 25 miles, nor could he identify all the formations being plotted – fighters, search aircraft, and the enemy dive-bombers cluttering up the short-range picture. The indifferent performance of IFF was the final straw. As the result of this accumulation of shortcomings, only eleven F4Fs managed to intercept enemy bombers before the D3As attacked, twelve others were involved with the A6Ms, and thirty did not come into action before the bombs fell. *Enterprise* was hit by three bombs, starting a

The 'Val Model 22' entered service in the autumn of 1942, in time to take part in the Battle of Santa Cruz, where great numbers were lost, but where the dive-bombers contributed to the sinking of *Hornet* and damaged *Enterprise*.

fire which burned for six hours and forced her to return to Pearl Harbour for repairs. Most of the D3As were shot down, including one shot down by a VT-3 TBF and seven by *Saratoga's* SBDs. The fighter pilots' claims were vastly inflated – thirty-nine out of thirty-two D3As and A6Ms – but one fact did emerge clearly: only five F4Fs were shot down by A6Ms, whereas the A6Ms' losses were for the first time higher.

Enterprise left Pearl Harbour after repairs on 16th October 1942. In her absence, *Wasp* had been sunk and *Saratoga* damaged by submarine attack, so that the only other American carrier in the area was *Hornet*, which had arrived after the Eastern Solomons action. *Enterprise* had embarked a new Air Group – CVG-10 – prior to departure; only the leaders were experienced pilots, 'new boys' forming the bulk of this first air group to be formed since Pearl Harbour being pilots newly out of training. On the other side, *Hiyo* and *Junyo* had been operational since mid-September, but their air groups were as inexperienced as CVG-10, as were many of the replacements who had joined *Shokaku* and *Zuikaku*. *Zuiho* joined the Fleet in October: the smallest operational carrier in the Pacific, she possessed only twenty-nine aircraft, but of these twenty-three were A6Ms. In total, the Japanese could deploy 113 fighters, eighty-one dive-bombers, and sixty torpedo-bombers against seventy fighters, seventy-two dive-bombers, and only twenty-seven torpedo aircraft aboard *Enterprise* and *Hornet*.

During the third week in October 1942, the Japanese Army on Guadalcanal made a major bid to capture Henderson Field. Close support would be provided by *Junyo* and *Hiyo*, while the other three carriers would guard against interference from the US Navy. In the event, *Hiyo* was withdrawn due to machinery defects and the shore assault failed. On 26th October, the day scheduled for the capture of the airfield, the two American carriers took on the more numerous Japanese force in the Battle of Santa Cruz.

Santa Cruz If anything, this battle was even more primitive than the Eastern Solomons action. The Japanese, fearing a repetition of a total disaster such as Midway, had taken to splitting up their carriers in widely dispersed formations, drawing false conclusions from the results of Midway and weakening their defence. The Americans retained their separate groups and their unco-ordinated strike organisation.

The defending fighters again failed to prevent ships from being hit. Successive pairs of VS-10 Dauntlesses found, reported and attacked Japanese ships, damaging *Zuiho*, but the A6Ms did not hit any of the search aircraft, while the latter claimed to have shot down ten fighters. The major strikes from the opposing sides met 70 miles from the American carriers and fighters from *Shokaku* and *Zuikaku* destroyed three F4Fs and three TBFs of CVG-10's attack wave, for the loss of one A6M. As in the preceding battle, the outgoing strikes and the incoming raid and returning search aircraft cluttered the radar plot, but on this occasion the *Enterprise* FDO lacked his predecessor's experience and was unable to achieve an interception before the enemy deployed to attack from two directions. *Hornet* had fifteen fighters airborne (out of the total of thirty-eight), and eight of these were used to intercept a raid heading for the other carrier, 13 miles away under the cover of a rain squall. From the time of this CAP's

'Tally-ho' onwards, the R/T discipline broke down completely and the FDO failed to re-establish control over the fighter force. *Hornet* was attacked by fifteen D3As and twelve B5Ns which co-ordinated their runs in a way which had not been achieved in any previous battle, and which attained the success it merited. The carrier was hit by two torpedoes and three 551 lb bombs; although she was taken in tow, further attacks inflicted damage and she had to be scuttled.

Enterprise was unable to provide fighter cover for *Hornet*, for only an hour after the attack the Japanese struck again. The second raid had been detected by the battleship *South Dakota* at over 60 miles, but *Enterprise* did not pick it up until the forty-four aircraft were in to 26 miles. Two dozen F4Fs were airborne, but few even saw the enemy before the attack began, and the D3As attacked unopposed, scoring three hits on the carrier; about fourteen B5Ns broke through the screen, and only skilful ship-handling saved *Enterprise* from their torpedoes – a destroyer was hit and damaged, and a cruiser hit but not damaged as the three torpedoes failed to explode. Not until the enemy began the retirement did the F4Fs engage in strength, claiming to have destroyed most of the bombers.

Only fifteen Dauntlesses of VS-8 attacked the Japanese carriers, the other aircraft delivering their torpedoes and bombs against cruisers and battleships in separate groups. At least twenty A6Ms intercepted the dive-bombers over *Shokaku* and the burning *Zuiho*, but they were able to shoot

Trailing smoke from its starboard wing cannon, a 'Zero' strafes *Hornet*, ablaze after a 'Val' had crashed into the base of the funnel. (*USN 80-G-40299*)

Above left.
A 'Val' heads for the water as another hits the wake of *Enterprise* during the Battle of Santa Cruz. (*US Navy*)

Above right.
A 'Kate' bores in to attack *Hornet* across the stern of a heavy cruiser after eluding the Combat Air Patrol. (*USN 80-G-20447*)

down only two SBDs and damage two others: the eleven undamaged dive-bombers persisted and scored six direct hits, destroying the flight and hangar decks but failing to inflict fatal damage. The Dauntlesses then fought their way out without loss.

Only twenty US Navy aircraft were lost in combat during the battle, most of them F4Fs shot down around their own carriers, but the Japanese lost more than half of the aircraft sent on strikes – about seventy out of 138 – as well as a number over Guadalcanal and the fighters shot down by the search SBDs. The failure to intercept the raids before they were delivered cost the US Navy dear, but the considerable losses sustained by the retreating enemy virtually destroyed the Japanese air groups. For the Battle of Guadalcanal in mid-November, the Japanese were able to deploy only *Junyo* and *Hiyo*, with virtually all the surviving front-line pilots in these two ships. As the US Navy had only *Enterprise* available, the latter avoided a carrier battle and all the air fighting took place over a Japanese convoy, where CVG-10 F4Fs and SBDs destroyed eight defending A6Ms for the loss of one SBD. The strike aircraft from Guadalcanal and *Enterprise* sank seven of the eleven Japanese transports and damaged all the others and ensured the retention of the island.

The last carrier 'battle' occurred on 30th January 1943, when G4M torpedo-bombers attacked a damaged cruiser off Rennel Island. The escort carriers *Chenango* and *Suwanee*, with twenty-nine F4F-4s between them, were providing close cover, with *Enterprise* within 50 miles. Three out of the twelve G4Ms were shot down, but the remainder closed in

Pilots had to be educated to use their IFF and to make sure that it was serviceable for every sortie. Cartoons such as this one from the US Navy monthly radio and radar training magazine were a common medium for putting across essential messages.

to finish off the cruiser and damage a destroyer. This unsatisfactory little brush only demonstrated again the fact that it was very difficult for an effective defence to be maintained over a unit separate from the fighters' base, whether ship or shore.

The Guadalcanal campaign was characterised by the courage and determination shown by both sides. In the fighting on the island, American numbers and superior technology inflicted complete defeat on the enemy; afloat, the victory was less clear cut. The US Navy lost two carriers, eight cruisers and fourteen destroyers; the Japanese lost only one small carrier, but their other losses included two battleships and four cruisers, and no fewer than 1,000 front-line aircraft. The Japanese carrier air groups had been formed only with considerable difficulty, by disbanding shore-based units and cutting short the normal training programme, and the relatively inexperienced aircrew had delivered effective strikes. The A6M pilots had not provided protection for either the strikes or the carriers and their kill: loss ratio against the Dauntless was in the dive-bomber's favour. The American fighter pilots had destroyed over 100 enemy aircraft, but most of their kills had been scored *after* the enemy attacks had been delivered. The A6M was a highly respected adversary, but superior American tactics had reduced losses in dog-fights to small proportions, particularly after the cream of the Japanese fighter pilots had been lost.

The Solomons campaign of 1943 saw no major carrier deployment by either side. The Japanese had their airfields at Rabaul and on Bougainville, and the US Marine Corps and USAAF possessed sufficient strips on Guadalcanal, the Russell Islands, and subsequent conquests to protect the series of amphibious landings. Distant protection for the New Georgia invasion was provided by *Saratoga* and *Victorious*, but the Japanese Fleet was in no position to interfere and the only fully-integrated US Navy/ Royal Navy task group saw no combat.

Dauntlesses over *Enterprise*. This photograph was taken in July 1944, after the Battle of the Philippine Sea, and on the carrier's deck, at the front of the deck park, can be seen two F4U-2 Corsair night-fighters of VF(N)-101C, which scored the first three true night victories by shipboard aircraft. (*USN 80-G-251063*)

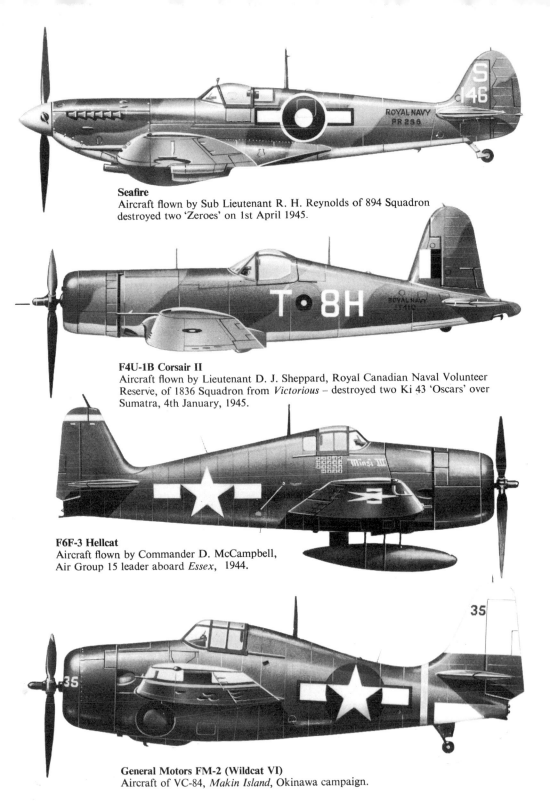

Seafire
Aircraft flown by Sub Lieutenant R. H. Reynolds of 894 Squadron
destroyed two 'Zeroes' on 1st April 1945.

F4U-1B Corsair II
Aircraft flown by Lieutenant D. J. Sheppard, Royal Canadian Naval Volunteer
Reserve, of 1836 Squadron from *Victorious* – destroyed two Ki 43 'Oscars' over
Sumatra, 4th January, 1945.

F6F-3 Hellcat
Aircraft flown by Commander D. McCampbell,
Air Group 15 leader aboard *Essex*, 1944.

General Motors FM-2 (Wildcat VI)
Aircraft of VC-84, *Makin Island*, Okinawa campaign.

5. Development and Doctrine

The New Fighters

The reconstituted air groups which embarked in the Japanese carriers before the Battle of Santa Cruz were equipped with a number of the latest model of A6M – the A6M3 Model 22. These had folding wing-tips for carrier stowage, a slight increase in internal fuel capacity, and forty more rounds for each of the 20-mm cannon. Most important, a new engine was installed: giving an extra 200 hp for take-off, it had a two-speed supercharger in place of the earlier engine's single-speed unit, to produce 1,100 hp at 9,500 feet, and 980 hp at 20,000 feet. In spite of being 600 lb heavier than the Model 21, the Model 22 was much faster in the climb and a full 20 mph faster at 6,000 feet and 20,000 feet. The maximum speed was 336 mph at 19,685 feet (6,000 metres) – considerably in excess of the Grumman F4F-4 and making it the fastest high-level fighter afloat.

The Supermarine Seafire – a naval variant of the Spitfire – saw its combat début on the same day as the Santa Cruz action. The first two Marks, the IB and IIC, were essentially medium level fighters, with sea level speeds of between 285 and 295 mph, and 350 mph (IB) and 330 mph (IIC) at 12-14,000 feet. The rate of climb of the British fighters was superior to that of the A6M3, and their high-speed manoeuvrability was also better; armament was very similar, consisting of two 20-mm cannon and four 0.303-in machine guns, all mounted in the wings. The Seafire family suffered from two major drawbacks, however: designed for short-range interception tasks, the Spitfire had barely an hour's combat endurance, and its undercarriage was designed for landings on long runways. Even when a 45-Imperial gallon drop tank was carried the Seafire had a patrol endurance of barely two hours, and its offensive radius of action was only 125 miles. In the spring of 1943, a low-level Mark entered service – the LIIC – with a speed of nearly 340 mph at 6,000 feet and a combat rate of climb of over 4,000 feet per minute. A year later it was followed by the LIII, which reached 356 mph at low level and possessed a startling acceleration. The weak undercarriage deficiency was never corrected, and more Seafires were lost in deck-landing accidents than through all other causes combined.

In the same month of October 1942, a brand-new fighter entered US Navy squadron service. This was the Vought F4U-1 Corsair, the prototype of which had flown in March 1940. The XF4U-1 was 100 mph faster than the F2A which had just entered service, but it was not the fighting machine which the US Navy had learned was needed from its observations of the European War. The aircraft was redesigned to conform to mass-production requirements and techniques, and the internal lay-out was completely revised. In consequence, the first production aircraft did not fly until June 1942, but sufficient were on hand by September to form a Marine fighter squadron.

The small saving in span bestowed by the folding wing-tips of the Models 21 and 22 of the 'Zero' was just sufficient to enable the aircraft to be struck down the lifts of the smaller carriers.

A clipped-wing Seafire LIIC comes in for a landing aboard HMS *Battler*, an American-built escort carrier. Removal of the wing-tips gave the fighter a very high rate of roll, enabling it to initiate changes of direction rapidly. (*FAA Museum*)

Below.

Although it was a 'world-beater', the Corsair was not adopted for shipboard service with the US Navy until 1945. The Marine Corps fighter squadrons profited from the Navy's reluctance and by August 1943 all USMC front-line fighter squadrons had been re-armed. Note the IFF reminder propped against the palm trees. (*USMC*)

The Corsair was probably the best all-round Allied fighter of its day. In its F4U-1A form, it had a maximum speed of 357 mph at 2,500 feet, and 405 mph at 19,500 feet, a combat endurance of four and a half hours with a 142 Imperial gallon drop tank, and a ceiling of over 35,000 feet. Armament consisted of six 0.50-in guns, with 400 rounds each, and two 1,000 lb external stores could be carried in place of drop tanks. The fuel tank ahead of the pilot was armoured, as were the windscreen, seat, and cockpit sides. The Corsair possessed a remarkable radius of turn – by dropping its flaps, it could stay with an A6M3 for the first half-turn at the latter's fighting speed, and could turn inside the British Seafire with ease. There were, however, shortcomings in performance and handling. The Corsair was a big bird: mean (fighting) weight with the drop tank gone was 11,359 lb – two tons more than the F4F-4 – and although it had 2,250 hp available when water-injection was installed, the weight resulted in a poor rate of climb – little more than 3,000 feet per minute. Rate of roll was also inferior to those of the 1942 British and Japanese fighters, and when it first appeared its deck-landing handling was not acceptable to the US Navy pilots. Not only was the undercarriage too stiff, resulting in severe bouncing on touch-down, but the large wing area led to 'floating' in ground effect over the deck, with a completely unpredictable wing-drop at the stall, the indicated air speed varying, as did the direction of the wing drop. This was sufficient to keep the Corsair out of US Navy embarked service until early 1945, but in mid-1943 the Royal Navy formed its first Corsair Fighter Wing, being obliged to use whatever modern equipment it could obtain. The wingtips were squared off to fit the folded aircraft into the lower clearance British carrier hangars, and this was found to eliminate the float and induce the stall at a constant speed. A small spoiler under the starboard wing ensured that that wing always dropped first, and modified undercarriage oleos were fitted. The Corsair Mark II went into action off Norway in April 1944, and three Wings saw action in the Pacific during the last year of the war.

The most famous Allied Fleet fighter of the war was designed after the Corsair but preceded it in US Navy shipboard service. The Grumman F6F was submitted as an outline design in early 1941, and 600 were ordered

The Corsair's long nose necessitated a long continuous turning approach to the deck, so that the pilot could see the batsman up to the moment of the 'Cut!', being given here by *Illustrious*' batsman to an 1833 Squadron aircraft. (*IWM A24279*)

Right.
The Royal Navy had four Corsair Squadrons operational aboard two carriers by April 1944. In that month, USS *Saratoga* (centre, on horizon) and HMS *Illustrious* combined to strike at Sabang, Sumatra, the former operating the Hellcats of VF-12 and the latter F4U-1B Corsair IIs of 1830 and 1833 Squadrons. (*IWM A24269*)

Opposite.

Left.
The Hellcat first saw action on 31st August, 1943, flying from *Essex* and *Yorktown* to strike at Marcus Island. This -3 bears the 'K' on the rudder and diagonal stripe on the fin to show that it belongs to *Yorktown*'s Air Group One, and the 'Top Hat' insignia of VF-1 below the windscreen. (*USN 80-G-474482*)

Right.
First victims of the Hellcat were 'Emily' shadower's from the Marshalls (*USN 80-G-175362*)

off the drawing board in that June. Before the XF6F-1 had flown, shortly after the Battle of Midway, the design had been recast, to give the aircraft an engine of 400 hp more, to increase the fuel capacity and the pilot protection, and to improve the handling. The XF6F-3 flew a month later, and was immediately accepted. The rate of production was such that the first squadron formed with the Hellcat in January 1943 and it was the standard fast carrier fighter by the end of August 1943.

Compared with the Corsair, the Hellcat was an unexceptional fighter aircraft. Between 25 and 30 mph slower at all heights, it was heavier, with a slightly lower rate of climb below 10,000 feet, and its endurance was greater mainly by virtue of its greater internal fuel tankage. The built-in armament and external ordnance capacity of the two aircraft was identical, but the Hellcat carried 50 lb more armour protection. The handling qualities were very similar, but the Hellcat had a distinct advantage in that it was much easier to land. The pilot was perched high on the fuselage, looking down over the engine cowling – in the Corsair, the pilot sat behind the $13\frac{1}{2}$ feet of cowling, fuel tank, and gun-sight which completely obscured the deck in a normal deck landing. The good view, clean stall and 'non-bouncing' oleos were decisive points in the Hellcat's favour. It became the standard fighter, and by being given the task of seeking out the enemy, the Hellcat pilots, with their superb discipline, training, and team work, were able to score more plentifully than the Corsair pilots, who were tied to land bases until the beginning of 1945.

The small slow escort carriers (CVEs) began to enter widespread service with the Royal Navy and US Navy towards the end of 1942. The former used Sea Hurricanes, Seafires and Martlets for the squadrons aboard the small carriers, these fighters possessing short take-off runs and low landing weights. The F6F-3, carrying the 125-gallon drop which was its standard load, took an extra 200 feet to get off the deck, compared with the F4F-4, and it weighed another two tons when landing, with a 10 mph higher stalling speed. The early CVEs' arrester wires and barriers could not cope with the F6F in conditions of low natural wind, and a lightweight fighter was needed. The only American fighter was the F4F series, and as an interim measure the F4F-4 was modernised, with improved R/T equipment, more armour, provision for heavier external stores, and gun armament reduced to four 0.50 ins. Built by General Motors, it was re-redesignated FM-1 and entered service with the US Navy and the Royal Navy (as the Wildcat Mark V) in 1943. The FM-1's performance was poor by 1943 standards – achieving barely 280 mph at low level, according to the Royal Navy – and its rate of climb was less than 2,500 feet per minute. In spite of its shortcomings, the FM-1 was the most numerous CVE fighter until the autumn of 1944, and it enjoyed a measure of success against Japanese and German bombers.

The final Wildcat variant was the FM-2 (Wildcat VI). The Martlet I and IV built for Britain had both been powered by the nine-cylinder Wright Cyclone, whereas the Martlet II, F4F-3 and -4, and FM-1 had all been fitted with the fourteen-cylinder Pratt and Whitney Twin Wasp engine, which gave more power at medium and high level, but was some 350 lb heavier than the Cyclone. The Cyclone Martlets were thus faster-climbing and had a better take-off performance, but were generally slower than the

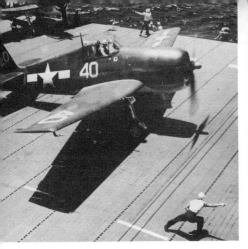

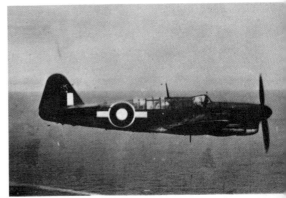

Twin Wasp Wildcats. In the FM-2, the Cyclone was adopted for US Navy use, the take-off rating increased by 100 hp, and the full throttle height rating (at 11,000 feet) by 190 hp. At the same time, the height of the fin and rudder was increased, to improve low-speed directional control.

The result was a considerable improvement on the FM-1: with a speed of 300 mph at low level, and over 320 mph at 13,000 feet, the FM-2 climbed to 15,000 feet in a minute less than its predecessor, having an initial rate of climb slightly in excess of 3,000 feet per minute. The reduced weight improved manoeuvrability, so that all-in-all the 'new' fighter was at least the equal of the A6M3 and its successor – the A6M5 'Zeke 52'. Produced in greater numbers than any other Wildcat variant, the FM-2 saw extensive service from 1944, operating from American and British escort carriers in the Atlantic, Mediterranean, and Pacific.

The last completely new Allied fighter to embark during the war was the British Fairey Firefly. Designed in 1939 as a replacement for the Fulmar, it was another two-seater. The first prototype flew in December 1941, but development problems delayed the formation of the first squadron until October 1943, and the aircraft was not cleared for combat use until the following spring.

The Firefly was a large aircraft, with a wing span of nearly 45 feet, but in spite of carrying an extra crewman, four 20 mm cannon with 640 rounds,

The FM-1 Wildcat saw virtually all its operational service aboard escort carriers, American and British. Not possessing a high performance, it saw extensive use as a close-support and flak suppression fighter.
P. J. M. Canter)
Above right.
The direct descendant of the Fulmar – the Fairey Firefly two-seat reconnaissance-fighter, seen here in British Pacific Fleet markings.

A6M5 'Zeke 52'
fighters aboard ship
in this instance the
USS *Manila Bay*,
transporting
Japanese aircraft
captured at Saipan
to Pearl Harbour.
(*USN*)

and as much fuel as the F6F, it was 1,000 lb lighter in the clean configuration. The engine was a Rolls-Royce Griffon in-line, delivering 1,735 hp at low level, and 1,495 hp at 14,500 feet. Although this was the most powerful engine to be installed in any wartime British naval aircraft, it was insufficient for the weight and size of the airframe. The Firefly's maximum speeds of 296 mph at 3,500 feet and 319 mph at 7,000 feet were therefore totally inadequate, as was its maximum rate of climb of 2,300 feet per minute. The take-off performance was surprisingly good – as good as that of the Martlet IV – and this was due to the Fowler-type flaps with their great

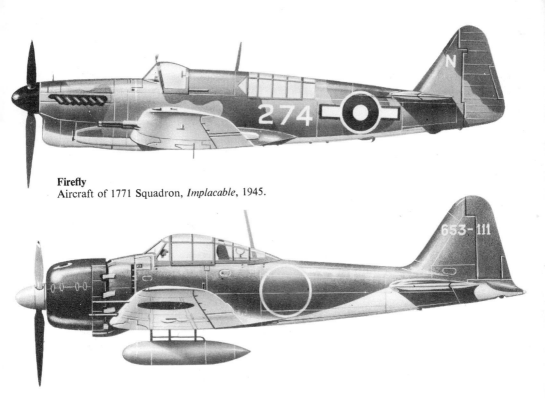

Firefly
Aircraft of 1771 Squadron, *Implacable*, 1945.

A6M5 'Zeke 52'
Aircraft of 653rd *Kokutai*, assigned to *Chitose*, *Chiyoda* or *Zuiho*, March to July 1944.

area. The flaps could be extended to an intermediate position to provide more lift without drag, to increase the cruising economy, and also to improve manoeuvrability. With extended flaps, the Firefly had a small radius of turn – almost as tight as that of the Hellcat, and with its light aileron controls this represented its main combat handling virtue. Regarded by the Royal Navy as a close support escort fighter, the Firefly was used primarily as an offensive flak suppression and strike fighter.

The A6M Type 0 remained the standard Japanese carrier fighter. A successor, the A7M 'Sam', was flown in prototype form, but difficulties with the engine, an earthquake, and the bombing of the factories combined to prevent its entry into service. To tide the IJNAF over the gap, the A6M3 was cleaned up aerodynamically, raising the maximum speed to about 350 mph at 20,000 feet. Faster-firing, harder-hitting 20-mm cannon were installed, and the A6M5 Model 52b featured a 13-mm (copied Browning) machine gun in place of one of the fuselage 7.7-mm guns. The 'Zeke 52' was introduced into service at the end of 1943 – slower in level flight and the dive than the Hellcat, its inexperienced pilots were no match for the US Navy and it made no great mark as a fighter.

Opposite.
Above left, right, below right.
The highly successful FM-2 Wildcat saw *all* its combat from escort carriers, such as the Royal Navy's *Searcher* (882 Squadron) and the US Navy's *Makin Island* (Composite Squadron VC-84). (*D. J. Frearson*) (*USN 80-G- 310925*)
Centre left.

A 'Zero 22' of the 2nd Carrier Division (*Junyo*, *Hiyo* and *Ryuho*) takes off from a Solomons airfield in April 1943, during the ill-fated Operation 'I-Go', in which the rebuilt Japanese carrier air groups suffered heavy losses.

Night Fighters

The need for carrier-based night-fighter aircraft did not arise as an urgent matter until 1941. The problems involved in locating ships at sea in darkness are greater than those in navigating to a city, and without search radar the reconnaissance and bomber aircraft were greatly handicapped. Only in conditions of bright moonlight, and when the last daylight position of the intended target was known with accuracy, could visual methods be employed, and then only by very small numbers of aircraft. Bad weather or low visibility also protected the ships and as attacks under such conditions were unlikely to succeed, fighters able to operate at night and in bad weather were not urgently needed. The ability of shadowers to take refuge in cloud was, however, an annoyance, and the Admiralty began to consider the employment of Fulmars as radar-equipped fighters late in 1940. At this time, Royal Air Force Blenheim and Beaufighter aircraft were enjoying some success against Luftwaffe night-bombers over Britain, and a modified form of their Air Interception (AI) radar sets was proposed for the Fulmar.

The Fulmar was in some ways an ideal aircraft. By night its low performance was less of a handicap, while its long endurance was a valuable asset. The second crewman would operate the AI, for there was ample room in the rear cockpit for the black boxes and radar displays. The first AI-fitted Fulmar began trials in 1941, and a development squadron was formed in mid-1942. The AI Mk IV was an early set, working on metric wavelengths; the radiated power was low, and the 'discrimination' poor, so that the maximum range against a bomber target was about two and a half to three miles, and the height and relative bearing information was insufficiently precise. The Fulmar was thus restricted by its radar and was used almost entirely for training, until an improved AI set could be developed for installation in a better aircraft. In March 1944, however, German radar-equipped shadowers and guided-bomb carriers led the Royal Navy to deploy two night-fighter Fulmar flights, each of three aircraft, aboard escort carriers serving on the Gibraltar convoy route. The menace decreased almost as soon as the Fulmars returned to sea, and there were no combat sorties.

The chosen Royal Navy night fighter was the Firefly, another two-seater with a sub-standard day performance. Centimetric AI Mk X had been developed for the Firefly NF Mk II, with the transmitter and receiver antennae contained in separate small radomes mounted on the inboard leading edge of the wings. The position of the antennae close to the fuselage and behind the propeller disc resulted in considerable blank arcs, and the synchronisation of the scanner 'dishes' proved to be difficult to achieve. The Firefly II was therefore abandoned in 1944, and a simple modification of the Firefly I, employing an American centimetric radar, was adopted.

Although the Imperial Japanese Naval Air Force had no radar-equipped aircraft in operational service during the first year of the war, the shadowers and attack aircraft displayed a remarkable ability to operate effectively in darkness. The US Navy therefore had a more urgent need for night fighters and a rather different approach was adopted. The Royal Navy, like the Royal Air Force, preferred that the pilot should be left free to concentrate on flying the aircraft while his observer, advised by a fighter direction

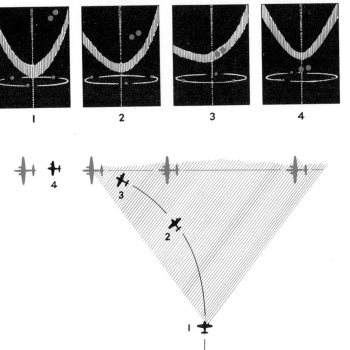

A straightforward 90° night interception:

The APS-6 radar screen in the F6F-3N 'office', situated immediately below the reflector gunsight and beside the Artificial Horizon (attitude indicator). With only six controls and an 'on/off' switch, the APS-6 was designed to be easily operated by a pilot who had also to fly the 'plane. (*US Navy*)

1. the target appears as a double dot at 45° to starboard, the right hand dot indicating that the target is above the fighter. The bright arc of light at about one mile range is the return from the surface of the sea. 2. As the target moves towards the centre of the radar display, the fighter pilot turns to port to cut the enemy's track. The pattern of the sea return changes as the aircraft banks, the unstabilised scanner 'seeing' the earth's surface at a shorter range to port than to starboard. 3. Still maintaining a converging track, the fighter closes to a range of one mile and the target passes through the ground return, the height difference reducing as the fighter climbs. 4. Tucked in below the target's tail at 400 yards, the pilot can see the outline of the target's wings on the radar screen.

officer, searched for the enemy and, after gaining contact, passed instructions and information by means of which the pilot could bring the fighter to a position from which he could look up to see the target's engine exhaust glow at a range of 300 yards or less. The US Navy had no two-seat fighters and no multi-seat aircraft with the performance considered necessary, and development was therefore devoted to the production of a pilot-interpreted and operated AI radar. To be fitted to a high-performance fighter with a minimum of weight and drag penalty, it was essential that a centimetric set with a combined receiver and transmitter antenna should be designed.

Much of the basic information on centimetric radar technology was obtained from Britain, as part of Lend-Lease, but the 'AIA' radar which appeared at the end of 1942 was entirely American, designed and built by the Massachusetts Institute of Technology. In January 1943, the Vought F4U Corsair was selected as the first night-fighter type to be equipped with AIA, and the first squadron formed, with twelve F4U-2s, in April 1943.

The first AIA (APS-6) installation on an F6F-3N; the radome's drag resulted in a loss of some 20 mph in maximum level speed at medium level. The 'T'-form antenna below the starboard wing-root is one of two AYD radar-altimeter aerials.

Left. The APS-6 scanner 'dish' at maximum deflection.

In September, six aircraft of the squadron, VF(N)-75, became operational from a shore base in the Solomons, scoring the first night Corsair kill during October.

By the late spring of 1943, a trial installation of AIA in the Hellcat was under test. Had the evaluation been entirely successful, the US Navy intended to order half of its F6Fs to be completed as night-fighters. This was soon realised to be impractical, for two reasons. In the first place, the radar could not be produced quickly enough to provide sets for every other F6F, and secondly the 29-week training course, for which only volunteers selected from the best Fighter School graduates and pilots with recent combat experience could be accepted, would tie up the pick of the fighter pilots for too long a period. Only 205 F6F-3s were built with fittings for AIA, and although two full squadrons were formed, VF(N)-76 and -77, they operated as four-aircraft detached flights aboard various carriers.

AIA was redesignated AN/APS-6 (Army-Navy/Airborne Pulsed Search Equipment) in January 1944 – a month before the first carrier deployments of F4U-2 and F6F-3N flights. The equipment weighed approximately 250 lb, the greatest part of which was the antenna pod, which also contained the transmitter and receiver and was mounted on the leading edge of the starboard wing. The radar employed a conical scan to provide azimuth and height information, and instead of the two separate cathode ray displays for the presentation of 'left-right, up-down' information, APS-6 introduced a novel 'double dot' method. Beside the true 'blip' generated by the reflected return from a target was a 'ghost', always to the right of the main echo, and positioned above or below (ie. at greater or lesser range), to indicate the target's relative elevation. The degree of displacement gave an indication of the extent of the height difference and although this was not as accurate as the more usual 'C-scope' information, it provided the simple raw data needed by a pilot who had to divide his attention between the radar and his flight instruments. The maximum range of the APS-6 was of the order of four and a half to five miles, and a target could be tracked in to as close as 400 feet range. A 'blind-fire' facility was also provided. By reducing the scan width from 50° on each side of the centre-line to a total of 15°, a continuous picture could be fed to a cathode ray tube in the gun-sight. The sight could be used within 1,000 yards, and as the range decreased so the image in the reflector glass assumed the form of an aircraft seen from astern – at the same time, the range was indicated to the

A Firefly Mark II night-fighter in an unfortunate attitude aboard HMS *Ravager*. The leading edge radome on the starboard wing can be seen, about two feet out from the fuselage. (*via J. Lambert*)

F4U-2 night-fighters of VF(N)-101 are brought to Majuro Atoll by a ferry carrier for transfer to *Enterprise* in February 1944. (*US Navy*)

Firefly NF I night-fighters of 1790 Squadron aboard HMS *Indefatigable* shortly after the war. The ASH (APS-4) radar 'bomb' can be seen slung below the engine radiator.

F6F-5N Hellcat
Aircraft of VF(N)-41, *Independence*, Leyte campaign.

pilot by means of a shortening line of light, the ideal firing range being 250 yards.

The Royal Navy was anxious to procure a number of F6F-3Ns, Britain being without a single-seat fighter suitable for carrying a lightweight radar, or, indeed, without the radar. The US Navy had a more urgent requirement and was unable to spare either a -3N or an APS-6, and the Royal Navy had to wait until January 1945 before significant quantities of F6F-5Ns were delivered. In the meantime, an AN/APS-4 ASH (Air-Surface 'H') centimetric radar was delivered to Britain and was immediately installed in a Firefly I for AI trials.

APS-4 was a remarkable piece of kit for its day. Weighing only 180 lb all told, its 140 lb scanner/transmitter-receiver pod could be slung on virtually any aircraft, and its junction box, control panel and indicator unit were small enough to be fitted in any combat aircraft's cockpit. Being designed originally for surface search, it had a wider azimuth scan pattern – 75° on either side of the centre-line – and a shallower elevation pattern – 30° above and below the longitudinal axis – than APS-6. In practice, however, the APS-6's 50° conical scan represented a theoretical coverage, so that the APS-4 was at least the equal of the 'custom-built' night-fighter AI in this respect, while its greater azimuth coverage made it greatly superior. The absolute maximum range was slightly less than that of APS-6, being four miles against a twin-engine target, but an experienced Observer could still make out the target at only 250 feet range. No blind-fire capability was available, but the APS-4's side-to-side scanning pattern provided a more accurately displaced 'double-dot' for assessment of relative height. The failure of the Firefly NF II had left the Royal Navy without its two-seat night-fighter, but the appearance of APS-4 enabled the Service to develop a simple variant of the Mark I, designated Firefly NF I. The first squadron did not form until January 1945, six months after the successful conclusion of the initial trial, and it arrived in the Pacific at the beginning of August, just too late for combat.

The United States Navy used APS-4 extensively during the last year of the war, fitting it to Grumman TBFs and Curtiss SB2C-3s and -4s, as well as to eighteen F6F-3Es and over 500 F6F-5Es. These night-flying Hellcats were search and attack aircraft rather than night-fighters, being used for intruder operations over airfields with considerable success.

6. Offensive

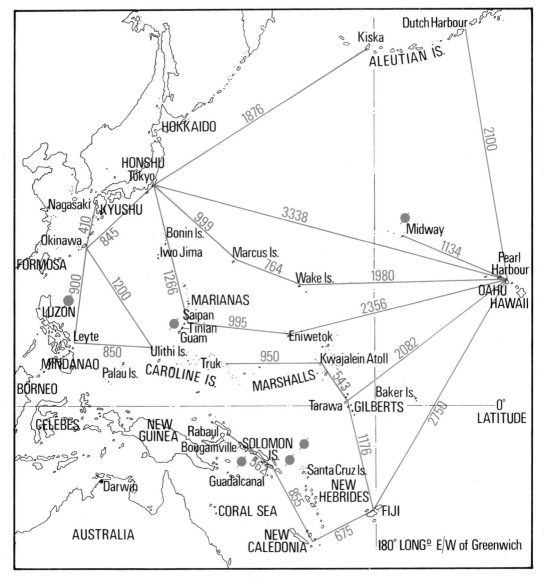

The Pacific theatre.   (Carrier Battles ⚓)

The Fast Carriers — 1943-44

While the fighter squadrons re-armed with Hellcats, the US Navy was commissioning and working-up its new carriers – the 27,000 tons, 33-knot *Essex*-class and the 11,000 tons, 32-knot *Independence*-class. The former were a logical development of the *Yorktown*, incorporating the lessons learned during the early stages of the war: capable of operating up to 106 aircraft, they were equipped with more up-to-date warning radar and with Very High Frequency R/T for aircraft control and direction. The smaller 'Light carriers' of the *Independence*-class had been ordered in March 1942 as an emergency measure, using a light cruiser hull upon which to build a hangar and flight deck structure. The Light carriers were thus related to the escort carriers, although their longer faster warship hulls allowed them to be used for Fleet work, with a complement of up to thirty-six aircraft, whereas the CVEs carried only twenty-five to thirty aircraft, their fighters usually being FM-1 or -2 Wildcats. None of the American carriers was heavily armoured against bombs, although the fast carriers were protected against torpedo hits by an armoured belt.

The aircraft complements of the two classes of fast carriers were decided in August 1943, less than a month before the first ships went into action. The *Essex*-class would operate thirty-six F6Fs, thirty-six SBD or SB2C Helldiver dive-bombers, and eighteen TBFs, while the Light carriers would operate twenty-four F6Fs and nine TBFs. A number of senior officers would have preferred to have eliminated the TBFs from the Light carriers, which would then serve as thirty-six-plane fighter carriers, but this was not approved for another two years.

The first operation involving the new carriers was the invasion of Baker Island, 650 miles east of Tarawa, on 1st September 1943. The Light carriers *Belleau Wood* and *Princeton* provided air protection for the operation and on D-Day their VF-24 and VF-23 Hellcats destroyed three H8K 'Emily' flying-boats so swiftly that the would-be shadowers were unable to make any report. Their base commander thus knew nothing of the presence of Hellcats or ships and grounded his remaining 'Emilies' in the belief that an unknown defect had caused the loss of the three.

On the same day as this promising start, Hellcats from *Essex*, the new *Yorktown* and *Independence* joined SBDs and TBFs in a minor (from the point of view of results) strike on Marcus Island – the first of the so-called 'training strikes' which were intended to blood the many new pilots and to enable the task force commanders to confirm the basic validity of their new operating doctrines. On 18th and 19th September, the new *Lexington* was joined by *Belleau Wood* and *Princeton* in strikes on Gilbert Islands targets; several ships were hit by bombs, and heavy personnel casualties were inflicted on the Japanese garrisons, but there was no air combat. Wake Island was the third target for the carriers, five of the six ships already employed taking part, with *Cowpens* taking the place of her sister ship *Princeton*. On this occasion, the enemy had fighters ready, but on 5th October the thirty A6M3 'Hamps' were badly mauled by the Hellcats in a combat over the target. A small raid from the Marshalls was turned away from the carriers, the Hellcats failing to score other than a moral victory. The enemy air opposition on 6th October was on a smaller scale, but a few

USS *Essex,* the name ship of the largest class of fast carriers to be used during the war. This view was taken during her shake-down in May 1943, with an Air Group Nine range of 18 TBF Avengers, 22 SBD-5 Dauntlesses, and, on the port side, ahead of the SBDs, 11 VF-9 Hellcats. (*USN 80-G-68098*)

A VF-5 Hellcat pilot opens up his engine to take off from *Yorktown* for the Marcus Island strike. Note the early-pattern plain star and the fairing over the inboard 0.5 in gun, dispensed with before the end of the year. (*USN*)

more combats occurred and Japanese losses for the two days came to twenty-two of the thirty-four aircraft based on Wake. Half-a-dozen American aircraft were lost to the A6Ms, and as many more to AA fire.

Rabaul *Princeton* had not taken part in the Wake Island operation for the reason that she had been redeployed to the South-West Pacific to join

Saratoga in strikes on air and naval targets in the Rabaul area. American forces landed on Bougainville Island on 1st November 1943, the two carriers striking at airfields on that day and the next, but without encountering Japanese aircraft other than shadowers. The Japanese Navy had robbed its carriers of their air groups for the second time that year, sending eighty-two A6M3s, forty-five D3A2s and forty B5N2s from *Shokaku*, *Zuikaku* and *Zuiho* to reinforce the hard-pressed 25th Air Flotilla at Rabaul; a similar deployment in April had cost the disembarked air groups over fifty aircraft and crews. On 1st and 2nd November, the Japanese carrier aircraft attacked the American beach-head on Bougainville, sinking one ship for the loss of about twenty of the 300 aircraft involved.

On 5th November, fifty-two F6Fs, twenty-two SBDs, and twenty-three TBFs from *Saratoga* and *Princeton* struck at Japanese warships at Rabaul. All but a handful of the Hellcats accompanied the strike, and to provide protection for the carrier force, which had launched the strike only 230 miles from Rabaul, shore-based US Navy Hellcat and Corsair squadrons from Segi Point and Ondonga (New Georgia) flew Combat Air Patrols. These were uneventful, but a new tactical concept was introduced by VF-33, whose Hellcats landed aboard *Saratoga* to refuel at the end of their first patrol and took off again to cover the return of the strike aircraft.

Seventy A6Ms were airborne over Rabaul when the strike arrived, but they were disappointed in not being given the opportunity to come to grips with the SBDs and TBFs. A division of F6Fs remained with each bomber flight throughout the dive on to the targets, providing close escort through the flak, where the 'Zeroes' were unwilling to follow. A small number of Hellcats remained above, to provide top cover over the rendez-vous for the attack formations, and these fighters were engaged by up to fifty Japanese fighters. The faster Hellcats were able to dictate terms to the 'Zeroes' which wished to press on, and about a dozen of the latter were shot down for the loss of three Hellcats. Flak claimed two more Hellcats, two Avengers and a Dauntless, and a VF-23 Hellcat returned safely to *Princeton* with over 200 holes caused by AA shell fragments. The bombs and torpedoes had severely damaged three heavy cruisers and damaged three more cruisers and two destroyers to a lesser extent. The only Japanese riposte was an unsuccessful dusk strike by eighteen B5Ns, which attacked two landing craft escorted by a motor-torpedo-boat (PT), damaged an LCI, and claimed to have sunk two carriers!

Rabaul was revisited on 11th November. Two carrier groups took part, *Saratoga* and *Princeton* launching their aircraft – fifty-five fighters, twenty-one dive-bombers, and twenty-five torpedo-bombers – from a position to the north of Bougainville, while *Essex*, *Bunker Hill* and *Independence* launched their seventy-two F6Fs, twenty-eight SBDs, twenty-three SB2Cs (in action for the first time) and fifty-one TBFs to the south-west of Bougainville. Again CAP was flown by the shore-based fighters, but on this occasion the Corsairs of VF-17 also landed on – aboard *Bunker Hill*, the ship to which the squadron had originally been assigned. VF-33 was divided between the northern and southern groups, twelve F6Fs in each CAP.

The *Saratoga-Princeton* strike arrived over Rabaul only five minutes ahead of the *Essex* group strike, instead of the 30 minutes intended. Sixty-eight A6Ms were ready for the raid, and some of these surprised the

American aircraft in the bad weather, destroying two and damaging five aircraft. The bad weather affected the accuracy of the bombers' attack and little damage was inflicted on the shipping in the harbour.

The full weight of the A6Ms' attacks fell upon the second wave of the strike, which was poorly co-ordinated owing to the lack of a commander-in-the-air to allocate targets and liaise with the fighter escort. The seventy-two F6Fs fought a series of dog-fights at various heights, destroying just six Japanese fighters, while thirteen American aircraft were shot down by the fighters and flak. One destroyer and four merchant ships were sunk by dive-bombers, but only two other ships suffered major damage, one of which had already been hit during the 5th November strike.

Saratoga and *Princeton* were operating in a belt of bad weather which had been partly responsible for the delayed strike and which prevented the Japanese from locating their group. The *Essex* group was 'in the clear', just 160 miles from Rabaul, and remained there in order to launch a second attack. The CAP aircraft of VF-17 and VF-33 had refuelled aboard *Bunker Hill* and *Independence* and covered the return of the strike and the carriers while the second strike was being prepared. As the escort fighters were being launched for the second time, at about 1325, a large raid was detected 119 miles distant – sixty-eight A6Ms, twenty-seven D3As and fourteen B5Ns inbound from Rabaul. The New Georgia-based fighters intercepted first, VF-33 meeting 'Vals' at medium level 40 miles from the carriers, while VF-17 –   at low level   – intercepted the B5Ns, claiming to have shot down eighteen in their first pass! The Japanese torpedo-bombers withdrew, reformed, and came in again. While they were doing so, the 'Vals' continued their approach in two separate groups, some reaching the carriers in spite of the large numbers of Hellcats and Corsairs attempting to engage. The A6Ms of the escort performed extremely well, for only seventeen of the dive-bombers were shot down by the CAP and the AA fire. *Bunker Hill* appeared to be the main target, but she was not hit by bombs and suffered only a few casualties from strafing. The surviving 'Kates' also broke through the defences and three torpedoes were released inside the screen, all missing the carriers; not one torpedo-bomber escaped.

VF-17 returns to *Bunker Hill* – an F4U-1 with the old 'bird cage' canopy lands aboard the carrier during the November strike on Rabaul. (*USN*)

Right.

Port wheel hanging down, a blazing A6M3 'Hamp' heads for the sea after running into the striking force's CAP. (*USN*)

The A6Ms destroyed three CAP fighters, but lost only two of their own number.

American claims totalled ninety-one 'confirmed' kills, bringing the day's score to 117 in air combat. In fact, the Japanese losses over Rabaul and the carriers were only thirty-nine aircraft. The US Navy pilots were still inexperienced and not yet able to get the best out of their aircraft in the first large-scale combats. The fighter direction organisation had been shown to have its deficiencies, for the D3As and B5Ns had managed to get through to the carriers in spite of the presence of over seventy fighters on defensive patrol. The close-range radar picture had become cluttered with the many aircraft inside 25 miles, and R/T discipline had again made identification and control unnecessarily difficult. On the other hand, the shore-based Corsair and Hellcat squadrons had integrated extremely well with the carrier defences and had been responsible for half the defensive victories. Although the two Rabaul strikes could not be hailed as great victories, they were a further step towards an efficient fighter defence capability, demonstrating the weakness as well as the potential.

The Japanese Navy lost heavily in these opening stages of the Bougainville campaign. As well as the damage inflicted on the ships at Rabaul, the aircraft losses were severe, and of the 173 carrier aircraft flown in on 1st November, only fifty-two remained to be withdrawn to Truk on 13th, with eighty-six of the original 192 aircrew. The greatest destruction had been wrought by USAAF B-25 Mitchell bombers, attacking the Rabaul airfields with fragmentation bombs and inflicting severe casualties among parked aircraft. The Japanese carrier force was thus faced with the prospect of training yet another generation of air groups, having lost the first in the summer of 1942, the second off the Solomons, and the third in the Rabaul area.

Gilberts A week after the second Rabaul raid, *Essex*, *Bunker Hill* and *Independence* (Task Group 50.3) were striking at targets in the Gilbert Islands, concentrating primarily on softening the defences on Tarawa Island in preparation for the assault on 20th November 1943. Task Groups 50.1 and .2 began operation on 19th, the latter attacking Makin – the other major assault target – while the former interdicted the enemy airfields in the Marshall Islands. *Saratoga* and *Princeton* (TG 50.4) struck at Nauru on the same day, and then acted as a covering force for the operation. Close support for the landings and local fighter cover was provided by forty-eight FM-1s aboard the escort carriers *Liscombe Bay*, *Coral Sea* and *Corregidor* off Makin, and thirty-six F6Fs from *Sangamon*, *Suwanee* and *Chenango* off Tarawa. All in all, the US Navy had deployed 440 fighters and 390 bombers aboard eleven fast and six escort carriers. Two more escort carriers – *Barnes* and *Nassau* – were carrying the forty-four F6Fs of VF-1, scheduled to be landed as a garrison air force as soon as Tarawa was secured. And this was only the first of the Central Pacific amphibious operations!

Against this powerful fleet, the Japanese could muster only forty-six operational aircraft in the Gilberts and Marshalls. A number of these were destroyed on the ground on 19th and 20th November, when aircraft from *Yorktown*, *Lexington* and *Cowpens* (Task Group 50.1) attacked Marshalls airfields. Designated the 'Carrier Interceptor Group', TG 50.1 was intended

View of *Lexington's* deck during the Gilberts operation. Hellcat '19' has two small 'rising sun' victory emblems under the windscreen, behind the VF-16 emblem. (*USN 80-G-426867*)

to provide a CAP barrier between the Marshalls and the Gilberts, but on 20th November it failed to detect a raid by sixteen G4M2 'Betties' which found TG 50.3 as *Essex*, *Bunker Hill* and *Independence* were recovering their last aircraft at dusk. The torpedo-bombers approached at low level and were only sighted as they split up for the attack. The F6Fs in the circuit destroyed a number of the G4Ms, but six of the nine which broke through the fighters attacked *Independence* and scored a hit which put the Light carrier out of action for several months. Eight G4Ms were shot down, the remainder escaping in the fading light.

The Japanese reinforced their Marshalls air strength during the days which followed, sending in thirty-two of the carrier aircraft which had left Rabaul on 13th November, as well as more G4Ms and A6Ms, for a total of sixty-eight fresh aircraft. TG 50.1 fighters intercepted an afternoon raid on 23rd November, destroying seventeen fighters and dive-bombers, and during that night and the next G4Ms harassed the assault shipping and close covering forces, without success. The defenders of the Tarawa Atoll were still holding out and inflicting casualties on the Marines, so that TG 50.2 was still in support when a shadower appeared shortly before dusk on 26th. The CAP shot down the aircraft, but not before it had made a sighting report, and as darkness fell other enemy aircraft were detected by *Enterprise*, *Belleau Wood* and *Monterey*. No night-fighters were embarked, but *Enterprise* flew off a CAP consisting of a TBF-1C Avenger of VT-6, flown by Lieutenant Commander J. L. Phillips, and two F6F-3s of VF-2, flown by Commander E. H. O'Hare and Lieutenant Commander W. A. Dean, the Air Group Commander and the Fighter Squadron CO, respectively. Only the Avenger was fitted with radar – a metric surface search set (ASB) based on the British ASV Mk IIN – which was unsuited for AI purposes.

The intention was that the two Hellcats should fly on the wing of the Avenger, which would lead them to the enemy, but in the event the fighters could not join up before the G4Ms closed in and the Avenger was vectored out alone. Surprisingly, Lieutenant Commander Phillips' radar operator did find a target and conned the torpedo-bomber into position behind a

'Betty', which was shot down by the two 0.50-in front-firing guns – the US Navy's first carrier 'night-fighter' victim. The sight of the blazing aircraft was the sign for Japanese gunners to fire wildly into the dark – the two Hellcats now came on to the scene and in the confusion Commander O'Hare was also shot down in flames, a tragic end for one of the Navy's finest leaders.

Tarawa was secured on 28th November, after bitter fighitng. VF-1 was flown ashore to take up the defence of the Gilberts, and the carriers retired to rest their aircrew and replace combat and operational losses. The next amphibious target was the Kwajalein Atoll, in the Marshalls, and to prepare the way for the operation and reduce the Japanese capability for striking at the Gilberts, two Task Groups struck at Marshalls targets, on 4th December 1943.

Marshalls While *Belleau Wood* and *Cowpens* provided the CAP over the force, ninety-one F6Fs and 158 SBDs and TBFs struck at Kwajalein shipping and the airfield on Roi Island, where the enemy had gathered nearly ninety aircraft. Fifty A6Ms were airborne to meet the F6Fs and TBFs over Roi, and all but twelve of the Hellcats became involved in combats which lasted for over half an hour and resulted in the destruction of twenty-eight 'Zeroes' for the loss of two or three Hellcats – the first really convincing victory for the new fighter. The dozen which did not take part in the air battle strafed the airfield, where nineteen other Japanese aircraft were destroyed on the ground.

The enemy retaliated at noon, and two flights of B5Ns – one of three and a second of four – surprised the carrier force by attacking at low level and missing *Lexington* by less than 100 yards. All but one of the torpedo-bombers was shot down by AA fire inside the screen – the seventh escaped. Instead of striking again at Japanese airfields, the carriers pulled out. Shadowers appeared at dusk and remained in touch for six hours, during which time G4Ms and B5Ns made fourteen individual approaches to the force, in two distinct waves. The first wave was beaten off by AA fire, but the second, in which the individual groups were larger, scored a damaging hit on *Lexington* putting her out of action for three months. No night-fighters had been available, and although *Enterprise* was present no attempt was made to employ TBFs for defence. The AA gunfire was particularly effective, however, and twenty-nine out of the fifty to sixty Japanese torpedo-bombers failed to return to their bases.

The Japanese possessed about 100 aircraft in the Marshalls on 29th January 1944, when the four carrier groups began pre-invasion strikes. *Essex* and *Intrepid* took care of Roi on the first and second days, destroying seven A6Ms just after dawn on 29th. These Japanese fighters had jumped F6Fs strafing the airfield and managed to shoot down four before the American pilots collected themselves to fight back. *Cabot's* CAP also scored, destroying six G4Ms which were trying to escape from Roi. By nightfall on 30th, eighty-three Roi-based aircraft had been destroyed (most on the ground) for the loss of eight F6Fs to AA and fighters. The other three groups had not seen any air combat, but had been able to concentrate on supporting the landings, backing up the eight escort carriers off Majuro, Kwajalein Island and Roi-Namur. The last named pair of islands were

Lieutenant D. Mulcahy, one of *Cabot's* VF-31 division leaders, was among the early Hellcat aces, and in January 1944 was recommended for the Navy Cross for his part in the air battle over Roi Island on 4th December, 1943. (*US Navy*)

secured on 2nd February, Kwajalein on 5th, but Majuro had been occupied without opposition on D-Day, 31st January. This last-named atoll became the advanced base of Task Force 58, the fast carrier task force, the first ships to enter being TG 58.2 – *Essex*, *Intrepid* and *Cabot*, on 3rd February.

Truk and after No attacks developed against the carrier forces or the transports and their cover inshore. The heavy Japanese losses in November and December 1943 and on the opening days of the Marshalls operation had included most of the remaining carrier aircraft, so that the Japanese Fleet, based at Truk Atoll, in the Carolines, was unwilling to interfere. As the enemy fleet was not prepared to come out and fight, Task Force 58 was ordered to seek it at base. The strike was foreseen by the Japanese: with the loss of the outer defences of Kwajalein and the Gilberts, Truk was exposed to attack, and so the major combatant units were withdrawn to Palau and Singapore between 3rd and 10th February. The air units, with about 365 aircraft, and much merchant shipping remained, for the purposes of supporting and supplying the remaining Japanese-held areas in the South-West Pacific.

Task Groups 58.1, .2 and .3 left Majuro on 12th February, five large

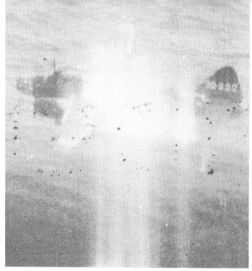

A dramatic photograph of a Hellcat chasing a 'Zero'. Part of a camera-gun sequence, taken by another Hellcat already firing at the enemy fighter, it shows a determined American pilot coming into the line of fire. Note that the drop tank has been retained, even in combat. (*US Navy*)

Above right. 'Betty' Shadower's last moments (*US Navy*)

and four Light carriers having on board 275 F6F-3s, 167 SBD-5s and SB2C-1s, and 127 TBF-1Cs and TBM-1Cs. In addition, *Enterprise* and *Intrepid* had embarked four-plane detachments from VF(N)-101, armed with F4U-2s, while *Yorktown* and *Bunker Hill* each carried four F6F-3Ns of VF(N)-76. The large carriers had each trained up a 'Bat Team' of an Avenger and two Hellcats following the damaging of *Lexington*, but this impromptu night-fighter force had not been exercised during the recent operation, and now it had been superseded by the first allocation of radar night-fighters to the carriers.

The carriers began launching the first wave of the Truk strike before dawn on 17th February 1944. To gain total air superiority, a sweep of seventy-two F6Fs was sent to clear the air and strafe the airfields. Japanese radar detected the incoming fighters, and about forty-five A6Ms and A6M-2N 'Rufe' floatplane fighters met the Hellcats. The American fighter pilots had now added technique to training and the result was a complete victory, with at least thirty of the enemy being shot down, for the loss of only four Hellcats. One of the most successful pilots was Lieutenant (Junior Grade) E. Valencia, of *Essex's* VF-9: with two wing-men, Ensigns C. Moutenet and W. J. Bonneau, he was flying top cover for two strafing divisions and was bounced by enemy fighters. During an almost continuous dog-fight which lasted until the Hellcats started for home, the three Hellcat pilots destroyed five 'Zeroes' and three 'Rufes', Valencia claiming three. His comment on his Hellcat was a classic: 'These Grummans are beautiful planes. If they could cook, I'd marry one.'

The air fighting went on through the morning, but by noon the air over Truk belonged to the Hellcats, which had shot down over fifty Japanese aircraft and, assisted by Avengers dropping fragmentation bombs, had destroyed or severely damaged 110 more on the ground. It was now the turn of the dive- and torpedo-bombers: protected by a blanket of Hellcats, they sank twenty-six merchant ships and four warships on 17th and 18th February, for the loss of just nine bombers.

The Japanese made just one attempt to strike back and it was successful. Half-a-dozen B5Ns approached the force after nightfall and their attempts to close were at first thwarted by long-range AA fire. When they withdrew,

120

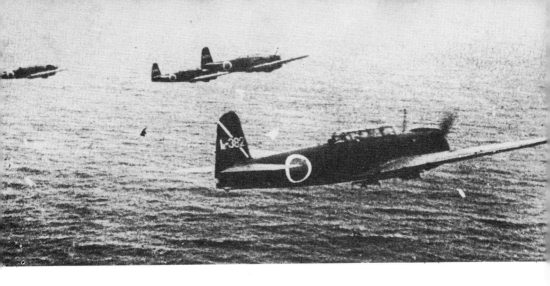

an F6F-3N of VF(N)-76B was launched by *Yorktown*, but the pilot and fighter direction officer lacked the experience to carry out a low-level radar interception and the B5Ns broke through and torpedoed *Intrepid*, the third carrier to be damaged by night torpedo attack.

The Truk operation was the second major victory for the Hellcat, which was shown to be superior to the 'Zero' when left free to fight, without the need to watch over strike aircraft. Henceforward, the fighter sweep was to be the principal means of protecting the strikes, clearing the air from the beginning and keeping it clear by maintaining Target CAPs (TARCAPS) over the area. Defensive arrangements were still imperfect – quite apart from the obvious night defence problem, the only daylight attacks on the fast carriers (off Rabaul and Kwajalein) had got through to weapons release, and the failure of the organisation was not made acceptable by the failure of the enemy to score hits!

Following the devastation of Truk, the Japanese concentrated the available strength of the First Air Fleet on the Marianas Islands of Saipan, Tinian and Guam. Task Groups 58.2 and .3 called at Kwajalein on their return from Truk and left after replenishment to strike at the Marianas airfields. The force of three large and three Light carriers was detected shortly before dusk on 21st February, when it was still over 400 miles from Saipan, and a stream of G4Ms attempted to attack over a period of six hours during the night. Four Corsair and eight Hellcat night-fighters were with the force, but no attempt to use them was made as it was realised that more training was needed before they could play a useful role. AA fire destroyed about ten torpedo-bombers and skilful ship handling prevented them from scoring a hit.

The fighter sweep on 22nd February was opposed by about thirty A6Ms and a number of J1N1 'Irvings', and there were also a number of attack aircraft forming up for a raid on the carriers. Twenty fighters and thirty-seven G4Ms and D4Y-2 'Judies' were shot down by the Hellcats, of which five were lost in air combat or while strafing airfields. Over fifty enemy aircraft were destroyed on the ground, but one of the most significant features of the attacks on the airfields was the destruction of the living quarters, where 250 Japanese aircrew were killed. The losses sustained by

The B6N2 'Jill' torpedo-bomber was potentially one of the most lethal aircraft in the Japanese carriers' 1944 air groups but although many broke through the Task Force 58 CAP on 19th June, 1944 the aircrew were insufficiently trained to take full advantage of their attacking opportunities.

the Japanese Naval Air Force during the previous three months had completely crippled the carrier force, as the aircrew of the Second Carrier Division (*Hiyo* and *Junyo*) had followed those of Carrier Division One to Rabaul and had suffered a similar fate. US fast carrier aircrew losses during the 1944 operations amounted to eighty-five pilots and crewmen, but spare aviators were already at Majuro and the pipe-line stretching back through Hawaii and the West Coast could supply the men without difficulty.

In March 1944, the Japanese began to reform their battered carrier units. An armoured carrier, *Taiho*, was nearly complete, and three converted ships – *Ryuho*, *Chitose* and *Chiyoda* – were available, enabling the formation of three Carrier Divisions, of three ships each. Air Group 601 had formed at Singapore in February 1944, for CarDiv One (*Zuikaku, Shokaku, Taiho*): a leaven of veteran pilots was available and three months were available for work-up with the newest aircraft types – A6M5 'Zeke 52' fighters, D4Y2 'Judy' dive-bombers, and Nakajima B6N2 torpedo -bombers. A6M5s were also supplied to Air Groups 653 (formed for CarDiv Three on 1st February) and 652 (formed for CarDiv Two on 1st March), but the take-off of 'Judy' was too long for the smaller converted carriers, and 'Jill' was too heavy for *Chitose* and *Chiyoda*, so that only *Zuiho* in CarDiv Three could carry the 327 mph 'Jill', the other torpedo-bombers in Air Group 653 being the old slow 'Kates'. *Hiyo* and *Junyo* carried twenty-seven 'Judies' and twenty-seven D3A2 'Vals' between them, but it was realised that 'Val' was too slow and too vulnerable to fighters to be effective, and so the main bomber strength of CarDivs Two and Three was provided by A6M2 'Zero 21' fighter-bombers, forty-five being allocated to Air Group 653 and twenty-seven to Air Group 652, for *Ryuho*.

The overwhelming majority of pilots in the newer Air Groups had joined direct from advanced training and had only the most elementary grounding in fighting tactics. CarDiv Two did not begin the embarked work-up until early April and the emphasis was on simple carrier drills during the month that was available. When the carriers were ordered to concentrate at Tawi Tawi, North Borneo, in mid-May, Air Group 652 had devoted little time to tactical training, its torpedo-bomber crews had not flown further than 100 miles from the carriers but were expected to be able to strike out to a radius of 350 miles, and communications procedures had not been sufficiently practised. The Combined Fleet lay at Tawi Tawi for nearly a month, awaiting the decisive battle; during this period the constant presence of American submarines off the anchorage prevented the ships from going to sea for flying exercises, so that the half-trained Japanese aircrew were thoroughly out of practice on the eve of battle.

While the Japanese Navy rebuilt its carrier squadrons, the US fast carrier force was adding to its experience by striking at Palau, where Hellcat sweeps destroyed nearly 100 Japanese aircraft on 30th and 31st March and the dive- and torpedo-bombers sank twenty-six ships. Three weeks later, between 21st and 24th April, Task Force 58 supported landings on the north coast of New Guinea: USAAF fighters and bombers had drawn the teeth of the Japanese Air Forces in the area, and although a few torpedo-bombers attempted to attack the carriers, they were either shot down by the Hellcats or driven off by AA fire at night. Truk was again attacked at

(Left to Right) VF-9
aces Valencia (23),
Bonneau (8),
McWhorter (12)
(*US Navy*)

the end of April, the Japanese having built up their air strength since February. A dawn sweep by eighty-four Hellcats was opposed by sixty-two A6Ms on 29th April, but the standard of the Japanese pilots was low and on this day and the next fifty-nine of the 104 aircraft at Truk were shot down by fighters and thirty-four were destroyed on the ground. Twenty-seven American aircraft were lost, most of them to the intense flak around the airfields. Task Force 58 now took a rest, to exchange Air Groups in some cases, and to exercise new carriers and Air Groups so that they could operate effectively with the Force. One offensive operation was undertaken during May 1944, *Essex*, the new *Wasp* and *San Jacinto* striking at Marcus and Wake Islands on 19th and 23rd May. The only significant feature was the use of the F6F-3Ns of VF(N)-77 for pre-dawn offensive patrols over the enemy airfields – without incident, as it happened.

The fighter direction organisation in Task Force 58 was not drastically amended, but improvements included better inter-ship communications facilities, in order to link the FDOs – one co-ordinating the activities of the Force CAP and one in each Group actually controlling that Group's CAP. Low-level raids were still liable to creep in under the radar, but Visual FDOs, controlling fighters at low level close to the screen, would be able to provide a last-ditch air defence capability. Visual direction had been pioneered by the Royal Navy during the August 1942 Malta convoy and it had proved to be effective against Italian torpedo-bombers. The fighter direction organisation for the escort carrier groups was slightly different. The CVEs were too small to accommodate the elaborate 'Combat Information Centre' organisation of operations rooms, fighter direction and filter facilities, and communications available in a fast carrier. The fighter direction was therefore undertaken by the amphibious force headquarters ships, which became responsible for the planning and performance of all air operations in the beach-head and invasion shipping area.

Saipan By the beginning of June 1944, when the US Pacific Fleet had assembled its forces for the invasion of Saipan, the fast carrier force consisted of seven large and eight Light carriers, with 443 F6F-3s, twenty-four F6F-3Ns, three F4U-2s (aboard *Enterprise*), 174 SB2C-1Cs, fifty-nine SBD-5s (on their last outing), and 192 TBF/TBMs. CAP and anti-submarine patrol during the approach of the invasion forces to Saipan, and close support thereafter, was to be provided by two escort carrier Groups, each with four CVEs, possessing 114 FM-2 Wildcats and eighty-two TBMs. In reserve, in the Eniwetok area, were five more CVEs, with sixty-eight F6F-3s, twenty-eight FM-2s, and thirty-nine TBMs, allocated to the Guam invasion force. Over 100 aircraft of all types were also at sea in Replenishment carriers accompanying the oilers of the logistic support groups.

Against this mighty array of embarked air power, the Japanese Combined Fleet had deployed 162 A6M5s, seventy-two A6M2s, ninety-nine D4Y2s, eighty-one B6Ns, and eighteen B5Ns aboard nine carriers. The strategy to be adopted for the decisive battle depended to a very great extent upon land-based aircraft, and since the February strike on the Marianas, the First Air Fleet had built up its strength in the area, until there were no fewer than 484 aircraft in the Marianas and 114 in the Western Caroline Islands. The Marianas could be further reinforced from the Home Islands via Iwo Jima. The carrier strikes would be launched from great range, attack American ships, and land on shore airfields. It would appear that nothing had been learned from the experiences of Rabaul, the Marshalls, Truk, the Marianas in February, or Palau: on each of these occasions, the carrier fighters had shown that by choosing the timing of the strike, they could dominate the air over the airfields and maintain daylight superiority, destroying aircraft on the ground wherever they could be located. Indeed, the Japanese had been the first to demonstrate the paralysing effect of a large carrier force, at Pearl Harbour, Darwin, and over Ceylon.

Task Force 58's four Groups left Majuro on 6th June 1944 (on the same day that the greatest amphibious operation of all time was being mounted from Britain against the coast of France) and launched 211 Hellcats and eight Avengers in a sweep over Saipan, Tinian and Guam on 11th June. A6Ms attempted to intercept Task Group 58.1 fighters over Guam but lost thirty of their number, while VF-28 (*Monterey*) Hellcats shot down six G4Ms over Tinian. Sweeps and strikes on the following three days were believed to have accounted for nearly 150 Japanese aircraft; the American estimate of the numbers available to the enemy at the beginning had been far too low, and it was believed that most of the enemy shore-based air strength had been eliminated. Two Groups, 58.1 and .4, were detached to strike at Iwo Jima and Chichi Jima, and on 15th and 16th June their aircraft destroyed about ten A6Ms in the air and nearly sixty Japanese aircraft of all types on the airfields.

Saipan was invaded on 15th June, but not until 17th did the first Japanese air strikes appear, from bases in the Carolines. B5Ns from Truk sank a Landing Craft (Infantry) between Eniwetok and Saipan, but in the evening seventeen D4Ys and two Yokosuka P1Y1 'Frances' torpedo-bombers, escorted by thirty-one A6Ms, attacked the transports and then the escort carriers. The forty-six FM-2s on CAP made few interceptions, due partly to the inexperience of the headquarters ship FDOs and the pilots, but also to the performance inferiority of the Wildcat to all the enemy aircraft. Two CVEs were near-missed, but *Fanshaw Bay* was hit and had to withdraw

Task Group 58.3 seen during the third day of the pre-invasion strikes on the Marianas (13th June 1944). *Lexington*, still with VF-16 embarked, had just returned after repairs, and with *Enterprise*, *Princeton* and *San Jacinto* (off picture) had 119 fighters and 110 strike aircraft available. (*USN 80-G-236892*)

from the operation. Eight of the enemy aircraft were destroyed by CAP and seven by AA fire, but most of the rest were able to return to Yap. Two small raids on 18th June failed to inflict any more damage on the CVEs, although an oiler was hit by bombs.

The Marianas Turkey Shoot At dawn on 18th June 1944, the Japanese Combined Fleet was 660 miles to the west of Saipan, and just under 400 miles to the west of Task Force 58, whose four carrier Groups rendezvoused at noon. Japanese aircraft from the carriers and from Guam searched for the American carriers, and the first contact was made during the early afternoon. The approach of the Japanese Fleet had been reported by American submarines, and Admiral Raymond Spruance, commanding the 5th Fleet, expected battle on 19th. Instead of heading west to meet the Combined Fleet, he coolly remained within 100 miles of Saipan, in position to defend the amphibious forces against a possible outflanking movement by the enemy. It has since been argued that the escort carriers could have protected the beach-head and shipping, but this ignores the losses suffered by the CVE fighter squadrons, the departure of *Fanshaw Bay*, and the

Below.
The second line of defence for the invasion forces off Saipan were the escort carriers. *Gambier Bay* was one of the small carriers attacked on 17th June, when the performance of the FM-2 pilots and ships' direction officers raised doubts as to the ability of the small carriers to defend themselves. (*USN 80-G-253809*)

indifferent performance of the CAP on 17th June. Spruance conducted a classic defensive battle, in the manner of the Duke of Wellington, choosing the position but giving his opponent the first strike.

Shadowers – D4Ys and E13A 'Jakes' – found the four carrier Groups and the battleship Group of TF 58 as early as 0530 on 19th June, the first on the scene being a D4Y from Guam. This aircraft achieved the doubtful glory of being the first Japanese aircraft to be shot down in the Battle of the Philippine Sea – *Monterey's* VF-28 being responsible. The shadowers suffered heavily during the day, twenty-three out of thirty-three shipborne reconnaissance aircraft being destroyed, as well as a dozen from Guam.

Over Guam, the dawn sweep discovered considerable activity, as Japanese aircraft were attempting to take off to attack the carriers and others were arriving from the Carolines to reinforce the island. Between 0825 and 0930, thirty-three out of the forty Hellcats over the island were in combat with arrivals from Palau, destroying thirty-five A6Ms and five bomber aircraft.

The first Japanese carrier strike, forty-three fighter-bombers, seven B6Ns, and fourteen A6M5s from CarDiv 3, was detected by the battleship *Alabama* at a range of 130 miles – 150 miles from the carriers. At this time, fifty-nine Hellcats were airborne on CAP and twenty-seven were on TARCAP over Guam. The carriers began clearing their decks of aircraft, to reinforce the CAP and to get the bombers out of the way: 140 Hellcats were launched and about thirty had to be recovered to refuel, so that there were just under 200 airborne at all heights between 30,000 feet and sea level to meet the sixty-four Japanese aircraft. To the surprise of the American FDOs, the strike began to orbit at a range of 75 miles while the leader of Air Group 653 briefed his followers on the execution of the attack, in which the torpedo-bombers were to break away from the main formation (at 18,000 feet) and descend to attack at sea level. The delay gave the FDOs time to vector out the CAP and forewarned by the R/T monitoring system they could block the enemy's play.

Directed by *Lexington's* FDO, eight VF-15 (*Essex*) Hellcats hit the A6M2s from 25,000 feet at a range of 70 miles. The B6Ns split away immediately, and were caught in their dive at 45 miles by six Hellcats of VF-25 (*Cowpens*); the new torpedo-bombers were too fast for the fighters, however, and only one was shot down before the 'Jills' left the Hellcats behind. Meanwhile, twenty Hellcats of VF-2 (*Hornet*) and VF-27 (*Princeton*) joined VF-15 in sorting out the 'Zeroes'. The A6M5s of the escort were unable to hold off the avalanche of Hellcats, which totalled fifty-six by the time that the remnants of the strike had closed to within 40 miles of the carriers. The latter were no longer the target, for the scattered groups of A6M2s and the six B6Ns were heading for TG 58.7, the battleships, 20 miles nearer.

The 'last-ditch' low-level VF-10 (*Enterprise*) CAP destroyed two A6M2s and a B6N just outside the AA barrage, but in spite of all the odds about twenty enemy aircraft made attacks. The only direct hit was a 550 lb bomb on *South Dakota*, and seventeen aircraft were claimed by AA fire. Two B6Ns, thirty-two A6M2s and eight A6M5s were shot down, for the loss of three Hellcats to the escort.

Ten minutes after the end of this strike, CarDiv One's strike was detected at a range of 115 miles. At the same time a shadower released 'Window' (metallic chaff giving a radar echo similar to that of an aircraft) to the north-west of TF 58, and the TG 58.1 FDO vectored out aircraft to investigate the spoof 'raid'. The 111 aircraft in the real raid began a 'pep-talk' orbit at about 90 miles, and again the Americans eavesdropped and vectored out CAP early. Thirty-three Hellcats were scrambled to reinforce the defence, but there were already over 120 fighters which had not yet been engaged, and eighty-one of these intercepted the enemy between fifty-five and thirty miles from the carriers.

First to attack were six VF-15 Hellcats, led by Commander D. McCamp-bell, who was to become the US Navy's top-scoring fighter pilot, with thirty-four victories. VF-15 harried the D4Ys for six minutes before the 'Iron Angels' of *Wasp's* VF-14 joined in, followed by twenty-three Hell-cats of VF-16 (*Lexington*) and eight of VF-27. The enemy strike had split into two main streams, one of which then divided again, but every group was intercepted, and seventy enemy aircraft were shot down for the loss of just four Hellcats to the forty-eight A6M5s of the escort. But again about 20 Japanese aircraft broke through, a torpedo-bomber crashing into *Indiana's* armoured belt, and six D4Ys attacking *Wasp* and *Bunker Hill* in TG 58.2. *Wasp* was slightly damaged by the fragments from an air-burst phosphorus bomb, and near-misses started fires in *Bunker Hill*: three of the six 'Judies' escaped. *Enterprise* and *Princeton* were both near-missed by B6N torpedoes, only the carriers' manoeuvring saving them from damage.

CarDiv Two's strike, twenty-five A6M2s, seven B6Ns, and fifteen A6M5s, flew to an erroneous position, but about twenty aircraft turned to search for TF 58 and these were detected by *Hornet* at ninety-nine miles. Seventeen Hellcats of VF-1 (*Yorktown*) and VF-2 (*Hornet*) intercepted the fighter-bombers at about forty miles, but the American pilots were remarkably unsuccessful and only five were shot down, as well as one A6M5 and a B6N. A few of the remainder pressed on and attacked TG 58.4, near-missing *Essex* by only 30 yards.

A second wave from CarDiv Two, reinforced by eighteen aircraft from *Zuikaku*, also flew to the wrong position. On finding no sign of TF 58, *Zuikaku's* aircraft turned back; during the return, the ten A6Ms sighted a search team consisting of two Avengers of VT-16 and a Hellcat of VF-16 and bounced the small formation, which was looking for the Japanese carriers. The 'Zekes' would have been better to have left the Americans alone, for they failed to hit and lost three of their number.

The Air Group 652 portion of the strike continued on to Guam and Rota. The latter contingent, of nine D4Ys and six A6M5s, sighted TG 58.2 and carried out an unintercepted attack on *Wasp* and *Bunker Hill*. The poor standard of training of the Japanese pilots was now made obvious, for all missed, and five 'Judies' were shot down by AA fire. The Guam-bound formation was detected by radar and forty-one Hellcats of VFs-2, -10, -15 and -25 caught up with the twenty-seven D3As, twenty A6M5s, and two B6Ns over Orote airfield. Thirty-five Japanese aircraft were shot down in five minutes and the other nineteen were damaged beyond repair.

Guam had been subjected to occasional attacks by the bombers launched to clear the decks. The Orote runways were cratered and put out of action for short periods, but the main effect of these raids was to keep the enemy

The slow 'Val' was still serving with the 652nd Air Group at the time of the Turkey Shoot, and here one begins to burn as the intercepting Hellcat scores hits. (*US Navy*)

Right.
A jubilant fighter pilot shows his score for the sortie to the camera. Unfortunately the identity of this one-trip ace is not known to the author. (*US Navy*)

heads down. After the massacre of CarDiv Two's second strike in the circuit, continuous fighter patrols were maintained over the island until dusk. Shortly before sunset, VF-15 made the last interception of the day, just as they had been the first into action against the enemy carrier strikes. The Commanding Officer, Commander C. W. Brewer, led his division to attack a B6N over Orote but failed to see a dozen 'Zeroes' which bounced the Hellcats and shot down Brewer and two of his wingmen. Brewer had already been credited with six aircraft destroyed and it is possible that fatigue was partly responsible for his failure to 'watch his Six'. Four other Hellcats and a Dauntless were shot down in air combat over Guam during the day, as well as two fighters and six bombers by the intense AA fire.

Night-fighter Hellcats patrolled over Guam and Rota during the night, but the only victories were scored by a pair of VF(N)-77A (*Essex*) F6F-3Ns, which picked off three enemy aircraft as they took off. A dawn sweep on Orote by Hellcats from *Essex, Cowpens* and *Langley* (TG 58.4) destroyed or damaged over thirty Japanese aircraft and forestalled a last strike from the land-based aircraft. This sweep marked the end of the Great Marianas Turkey Shoot – the greatest air battle of the war.

The Combined Fleet had launched 373 aircraft in four strikes, as well as thirty-three shadowers. Of these, 243 were lost and over thirty returned with severe damage. Two carriers had been torpedoed by American submarines and were lost as a result of their poor design: *Taiho* and *Shokaku* took another twenty-two aircraft down with them. At dawn on 20th June, the seven remaining carriers had only sixty-eight A6M5s and A6M2s, three D4Ys, and twenty-nine B6Ns and B5Ns serviceable. The Guam air strength was exhausted, for the fighters had destroyed fifty-eight land-based aircraft in the air, fifty-two more had been destroyed on the ground, and many more were damaged beyond repair. Of the 298 Japanese aircraft shot down on this day, over 250 had fallen to the Hellcats, 295 of which had engaged the enemy. Fourteen Hellcats were shot down by aircraft, as well as the single Dauntless. American losses overall came to only thirty aircraft, of which six were not due to enemy action. Thanks to the efficient

Commander David McCampbell, Air Group 15 Commander, seen in his 'Minsi III', with 19 victory flags, taxies up *Essex's* flight deck. (*US Navy*)

rescue service, seventeen of the forty-four aircrew were rescued – over 400 Japanese aircrew died.

And yet Task Force 58 had had a narrow escape. For all the success of the fighter squadrons, over fifty Japanese aircraft had got through to attack the ships and had damaged two carriers and two battleships – none seriously. Had the bomber pilots been endowed with the expertise of the 1942 breed of Japanese pilots, then the 14.3 per cent penetration rate would have proved to be extremely costly to the US Navy. The weather had been perfect for the defence, radar had given excellent detection ranges, and the Japanese strike leaders had broadcast their plans of attack, but dive-bombers and torpedo-bombers had still got through to their targets, in spite of the poor training of the crews. When formations had been intercepted they broke up, and the Hellcats, fighting in two- and four-plane units, could not deal with all of the enemy aircraft. With such a tangle of radar contacts, friendly and hostile, the FDOs could not always sort out the identity of each group, and R/T discipline, as ever, began to deteriorate in proportion to the length of the combat, pilots making unnecessary calls and blocking the more important information transmissions as to enemy movements and numbers. The A6M5s had managed to tie up some of the fighters, but suffered heavily in the process; on the other hand, very few B6Ns had been stopped – 'Jill' was a very dangerous lady, who could out-dive and out-turn even the Hellcat.

On 20th June, Task Force 58 turned to pursue the Combined Fleet and delivered its counter-strike half-an-hour before sunset. Forty A6Ms were airborne to defend the Japanese Fleet against the eighty-five Hellcats, seventy-seven dive-bombers and fifty-four Avengers. The defending pilots showed considerable skill, holding off the Hellcats and attacking the bombers in spite of being so outnumbered. Six Hellcats, four Avengers,

VF(N)-77B night-fighter Hellcats stand by on deck while down in *Yorktown*'s hangar Air Group One ordnance men prepare 1,000 lb bombs for the next day's strike on the Japanese, with a background of off-duty crewmen watching a movie. Hellcat '00' is the mount of Commander J. M. Peters, the Air Group Commander.

and ten SB2C Helldivers were shot down by the 'Zeroes', which lost twenty-five of their number shot down and nine badly damaged. *Hiyo* was torpedoed and sunk, *Zuikaku* was heavily damaged, and *Chiyoda* and *Ryuho* were less badly damaged by the striking aircraft. Returning in the dark, eighty American aircraft were lost through fuel exhaustion and accidents. Only forty-nine of the 209 aircrew involved were lost.

The Big Blue Blanket — 1944-45

The Philippines After the failure of the Combined Fleet to achieve any success against the American forces off the Marianas, the Japanese high command gave no more assistance to their garrisons, and by 10th August Saipan, Tinian and Guam were under American control. In July, the process of rebuilding the carrier air groups began again, but the training was slow due to the lack of experienced instructors and a shortage of aviation fuel. Time was needed to produce a force which would be a qualitative match for the US Navy, and as time was not available the Japanese were forced to opt for quantitative parity. The Japanese Naval Air Force had remaining about 900 front-line attack aircraft and crews, based in the Home Islands, Formosa, and the Philippines, and over 200 Army Air Force aircraft were under Naval command in the Formosa area, as well as another 250 in the Philippines. Task Force 58, with over 800 aircraft, would nearly always outnumber the Japanese air opposition because it was concentrated, whereas the enemy had to disperse his aircraft throughout his contracting Empire.

American fast carrier groups struck at Iwo Jima, Yap, and Palau during the latter stages of the Marianas campaign, and in mid-September the whole force covered the invasion of the Palau Islands. Eight large and eight Light carriers attacked Japanese airfields in the Southern Philippines before the invasion (15th September 1944), claiming to have destroyed 168 enemy aircraft in air combat and over 200 on the ground, for the loss of twenty-two F6Fs, SB2Cs and TBMs.

Attacks on Luzon on 21st and 22nd September were not seriously opposed – Japanese Army and Air Force fighters were brushed aside by the Hellcats, although the potential of such new fighters as the Kawanishi N1K1-J 'George' and Nakajima Ki 84 'Frank' was noticed by the US Navy pilots. Had sufficient numbers been available, and the trained pilots to fly them, then the Hellcat would at last have found a dangerous challenge. Three hundred Japanese aircraft were claimed as destroyed during the two days, most of them on the ground.

The fighter squadrons were now receiving F6F-5 Hellcats, with their F6F-5N night counterparts. The main performance increase was at low level, where the -5 was 15 mph faster than the -3; the slight increase in weight actually reduced the rate of climb. The main advantage of the -5 was its increased versatility. The -3 had been able to carry bombs and, after modification, rocket projectiles, but the new aircraft had the wiring installed for all roles; after June 1944, all aircraft leaving the production lines were also modified for the night-fighter role, lacking only the scanner and black boxes, which could be fitted on board the carriers. An additional device for the night-fighter was the APS-13 tail-warning radar, which gave warning of an aircraft within 60° of the fighter's tail at a range of 800 yards. The fitting of radar gear reduced level speed by about 20 mph and the rate of climb suffered, but the penalty of carrying the 'zero-length' R/P stub launchers – common practice from September 1944 – was even greater.

The night-fighting potential of the fast carrier force (redesignated Task Force 38 under the command of Admiral W. F. Halsey) had been greatly increased in August by the arrival of *Independence*, armed and worked-up as a night carrier, with five day-fighter F6Fs, fourteen F6F-5Ns and eight APS-4-equipped TBM-1D Avengers. The detachments aboard the large carriers had been amalgamated with the fighter squadrons of those ships, so that there were forty-one -3Ns and -5Ns in addition to those aboard *Independence*. The 'day carriers' were, however, loth to use their night-fighters – working hard between dawn and dusk, the hours of darkness were needed to rest men and maintain machines, many of which had to remain on deck throughout the period at sea. Every night launch and recovery would entail shifting the entire deck park – a routine that could not be maintained throughout the 24 hours indefinitely. *Independence* flew little by day and was manned and equipped for intensive night operations.

Formosa On 10th October, Task Force 58 launched 1,396 sorties against Okinawa and other Ryukyu Islands airfields. The Japanese took this on-slaught to be the overture to the invasion of either Formosa or Leyte, in the Philippines, and moved aircraft to the former to repel the assault. Included in the reinforcements were 250 of the half-trained pilots of the latest carrier generation. In fact, Leyte was to be the target for the invasion, but Task Force 38 would first neutralise Formosa as a base and staging post.

Admiral Halsey took his nine large and seven Light carriers to within 100 miles of Formosa on 12th October, beginning the day with the usual fighter sweeps. The Hellcats from all four groups met stronger opposition than they had experienced for several months, for nearly 200 fighters attempted to interfere. Over 100 Japanese aircraft were shot down in the fighting, but Hellcat losses were also heavy, more than thirty being shot down, and losses for the day rose to forty-eight thanks to the AA defences of the airfields. Sixty Japanese fighters met the second strike and lost so heavily that no attempt was made to oppose the third.

Task Force 38 was not attacked until nightfall, when G4M torpedo-bombers attempted to parallel their earlier successes. *Independence's* VF(N)-41 gratefully took the chance and destroyed five 'Betties' during the four hours up to midnight, stalking and destroying one bomber after another. Two kills were scored by Lieutenant W. E. Henry, who was to become the squadron's leading marksman, with six night victories.

The strikes on Formosa were renewed on 13th October and more enemy aircraft were destroyed in the air and on the airfields. At dusk, however, four G4Ms made an undetected attack on TG 38.4, narrowly missing *Franklin* with torpedoes. One bomber attempted to crash the carrier but skidded across the deck and fell in the sea. Task Group 38.1 was also attacked and the heavy cruiser *Canberra* was torpedoed. The remainder of the sortie was devoted to extricating the crippled cruiser, which was given close escort by *Cowpens* and *Cabot*. The cruiser *Houston* was also damaged, at dusk on 14th October, and had to be towed out in the same group as

Canberra. Task Group 38.4 struck at the Manila area on 15th but during the forenoon a small Japanese strike managed to evade the CAP and a D4Y scored a hit on *Franklin*, causing slight superficial damage. An afternoon repeat performance, by ninety aircraft, was completely routed by the CAP. The last major raid was launched against the 'Cripple Division' on 16th October. VF-22 and VF-29, with only forty-six F6Fs between them, destroyed twenty-seven out of the 107 Japanese aircraft and drove off most of the remainder. Inevitably, three got through and a P1Y1 'Frances' torpedoed *Houston* again.

The first 'night carrier', USS *Independence*, seen just before the Formosa strikes, with the -5N Hellcats and TBM-1D Avengers of Night Air Group 41 ranged on deck. (*USN 80-G-284101*)

The Japanese Navy admitted the loss of 492 aircraft during the week, and it is probable that the Army lost another 150. The loss of most of the carrier aircraft in this battle left the one operational CarDiv (*Zuikaku*, *Zuiho*, *Chitose* and *Chiyoda*) with fifty-two A6M5s, twenty-eight A6M2 fighter-bombers, twenty-five B6N2s, four B5N2s, and seven D4Y2s. At this time, *Essex* alone was carrying fifty Hellcats, twenty-five Helldivers and twenty Avengers, and she was but one of nine large carriers taking part in the Leyte campaign.

Leyte – the Kamikazes Close cover for the assault was provided as usual by the escort carriers – eighteen of them, armed with eighty-five Hellcats, 219 Wildcats and 199 Avengers. In addition to softening up the beach-head, the escort carrier aircraft also undertook fighter sweeps and strikes over the Central Philippines, enjoying an unusual freedom and destroying most of the remaining Japanese air strength south of Leyte. From 'A'-Day, 20th October 1944, one CVE Group (TG 77.4) maintained a continuous Hellcat and Wildcat CAP over Leyte Gulf, with sixteen aircraft on station and twice as many at immediate readiness on deck. The proximity of land all around the shipping anchorage cluttered the fighter direction ships' radar screens so that little warning of the approach of enemy aircraft was obtained and giving the CAP pilots little chance of intercepting before the enemy aircraft could strike. A cruiser was torpedoed on 'A'-Day and another was crashed on 21st, but not until 24th did the enemy appear in numbers.

Only two fast carrier groups had been on hand at the beginning of the invasion, and these were unable to interdict the Luzon airfields as well as maintain cover for the inshore groups, and the Japanese had thus been able

Opposite.

The light cruiser
Birmingham closes
the burning
Princeton to take off
men not required for
fighting the Light
carrier's fires. While
the two ships were
close together,
Princetown's torpedo
magazine blew up,
killing and wounding
600 of the cruiser's
personnel. (*US Navy*)

to fly in reinforcements. On 24th October, between 150 and 200 aircraft, out of the 400 in the Philippines, attacked the beach-head area. The fast carriers were away striking at the main Japanese battle fleet in the Sibuyan Sea, and the CVEs provided all the Leyte CAP, maintaining twelve FM-2s in the air but frequently scrambling the two dozen held at readiness. The Wildcat pilots took advantage of a unique opportunity and claimed to have destroyed sixty-six assorted Japanese aircraft, at negligible cost to themselves.

The fruitless attacks on the Leyte shipping were part of the 'Sho' Operation, intended to inflict a major defeat on the American forces. The battleship force proceeding through the Sibuyan Sea was to be one of two striking forces which would seek to destroy ships in Leyte Gulf; the weak carrier force was heading down the east side of Luzon, acting as bait to draw off Task Force 38, which was to be attacked by land-based aircraft and the one strike which the carriers would be able to launch.

Three groups of TF 38 were now present, and TG 38.3 (*Essex, Lexington, Princeton* and *Langley*) were approached by three raids, each consisting of between fifty and sixty aircraft. One raid was intercepted by Commander McCampbell and seven VF-15 pilots: the bomber formations were broken up and dispersed, but the escorting fighters went into a defensive circle, although they greatly outnumbered their opponents. The Hellcat pilots tormented the Japanese for *ninety minutes*, picking off any pilot careless enough to stray out of the circle, and when the carrier pilots had to break off as they were running short of fuel, their 'bag' came to twenty-five – nine to McCampbell, six to Lieutenant(jg) R. W. Rushing, and the remainder shared between the other six Hellcat pilots.

The other raids were also broken up and the defence was helped by the cloud in the area, which concealed the ships from the medium level raids. Unfortunately, it gave cover to one determined D4Y, which followed a CAP division home, waited among the clouds until *Princeton* began to recover her aircraft, and then scored a direct hit with a 551 lb bomb. Two years had elapsed since an American carrier had been hit squarely in a daylight attack, and the blow was fatal (as it had been on the previous occasion), for the Light carrier caught fire and had to be scuttled. She was to be the last American fast carrier to be sunk.

The last Japanese carrier strike was launched shortly before noon on 24th October and consisted of forty A6M5s, twenty-two A6M2s, six B6Ns and six D4Ys. *Lexington's* CAP was vectored out and intercepted the strike above the clouds, which gave cover to the dispersed Japanese aircraft, most of which diverted to airfields ashore. Only the six 'Judies' remained together and pressed on to attack TG 38.3 without success.

Hellcats of TF 38 distinguished themselves during the night and the following day. F6F-5Ns from *Independence* backed up the TBM-1D shadowers watching the Japanese carriers during the night, and on 25th all four were sunk in the 'Battle' of Cape Engaño, Commander McCampbell acting as Air Co-ordinator for the first strike.

But while Halsey's eleven fast carriers and six battleships chased the bait, the main Japanese force broke out through the unguarded San Bernadino Channel between Luzon and Samar. At dawn the four battleships and six heavy cruisers fell upon the six escort carriers of Task Unit

1: *Suwanee* under Kamikaze attack, 26th October, 1944 a suicide 'Zero' dives steeply on the carrier as a second runs in strafing the AA guns, pursued, far left, by an Avenger. (*USN 80-G-*)

2: The fireball of the Kamikaze hit

3: and the cloud of smoke from the explosion; the escort 'Zero' turns away, still pursued by the aptly-named Avenger.

4: Almost dead in the water, *Suwanee* fights the fire. Two hours later, with the 10-feet diameter hole in the forward flight deck patched and all fires out, she was operating aircraft. (*USN 80-G-270621*)

77.4.3, to the mutual surprise of both sides. The 18-knot CVEs, escorted by seven destroyers and destroyer-escorts, were under fire for two and a half hours before the enemy broke off the action due to the repeated attacks from the carriers' aircraft, which sank two heavy cruisers, for the loss of twelve Avengers and eleven Wildcats to AA fire. One carrier, *Gambier Bay*, was sunk by shell-fire and four others were damaged.

Even as this epic battle was being fought, the Japanese First Air Fleet played what was intended to be the trump card. About 30 miles to the south of TU 77.4.3, the four escort carriers of TU 77.4.1 had just completed launching a strike to assist .4.3 when, at 0740, an A6M dived almost vertically on *Santee*, hitting her forward and going through the flight deck into the hangar. The fires were under control by 0751, but five minutes later she was torpedoed by the submarine *I-56* – a rare and fortuitous example of a combined attack by the Japanese. In the meantime, *Sangamon* and *Petrof Bay* had also been attacked, but narrowly missed by suicidal A6Ms. At 0800, *Suwanee* was hit in the middle of the deck, but again the fires were quickly subdued and the patched deck was ready for landings two hours later. The two CVEs survived their hits: the *Sangamon*-class converted oilers were the largest and strongest escort carriers, and it was unfortunate for the suicide pilots that they should have chosen these as targets for the first Kamikaze attacks.

The idea of organised suicide units had been first mooted after the Battle of the Philippine Sea. Conventional attacks had achieved nothing but the loss of aircraft – if the aircraft were to be lost, then why not in crashes on the targets. Not only did the warrior creed of Bushido glorify death in battle, but the pilot half-expecting to be caught by the efficient US Navy defences in a normal attack would now press on and not be turned back at the sight of fighters. There was initial opposition from the Naval Staff, but training of the first 'Special Attack Units' began in the Philippines during the autumn of 1944, and after the failure of the Formosa-based bombers to inflict serious damage on Task Force 38 in mid-October it was realised that the Kamikaze would have to become the major anti-carrier weapon.

Tactics were devised to take full advantage of the known weaknesses in the American defences. After two and a half years, the Japanese had a very clear idea of the radar coverage and the gaps above and below the 'lobes', which could be exploited by approach at very great or very low altitudes. By monitoring R/T traffic between aircraft and ships, it had been discovered that the Task Force usually employed only two interception frequencies, with up to twenty CAP divisions being controlled on them. By flying many diversionary sorties, with aircraft flying zig-zag tracks, and constantly changing heights and speeds, the CAPs could be drawn out to investigate, thus cluttering up the radar and the R/T channels, while the true attackers, in small groups, or even singly, made their undetected approaches. The high-level run-in was regarded as being the more difficult for the almost vertical dive in the radar's overhead blind spot resulted in a high terminal velocity, giving the pilot less time to make last minute corrections to deal with evasive measures by the target. The low-level approach had two variations: the aircraft could either zoom to about 10,000 feet and then dive steeply on the target, or it could climb to less than 5,000 feet for a shallow-angle attack. In general, the latter was preferred, for the steep dive needed good weather and considerable pilot skill, both for judging the range at which to pull up and for the dive, whereas even inexperienced pilots could make corrections for target movement and the effect of the wind in a slower attack at an angle which could be steepened or made flatter without difficulty. The aiming point was to be the centre of the flight deck of carriers, abreast the island; other types of ship were to be crashed at the base of the bridge structure.

The four Kamikazes which had attacked *Santee*, *Suwanee* and *Petrof*

A Kamikaze 'Zeke' prepares for take-off, a 554 lb Type 99 semi-armour-piercing bomb fixed under the fuselage.

A VF-20 F6F-5 lands aboard *Lexington* during the Philippines campaign. (*US Navy*)

Bay had not been detected by radar and had struck out of a clear sky. Three hours later, five more, escorted by four A6M5 fighters, attacked TU 77.4.3: *Kitkun Bay* had one bounce off her port deck-edge into the sea where the bomb carried by the A6M exploded underwater and caused severe damage to the hull.

Simultaneously, *White Plains* was near-missed by a shallow attack from astern, and *St Lo* was hit squarely on the flight deck – the Kamikaze exploded in the hangar, causing fires which detonated bombs loaded on Avengers. She sank 30 minutes after the attack. While the screen was recovering men from the water, two more suicide aircraft, D4Ys, attacked, scoring a hit on *Kalinin Bay*, causing a fire on her flight deck, and crashing close to *Kitkun Bay* and adding to the latter's underwater damage. A pair of FM-2s from *Kitkun Bay's* Composite Squadron (VCS-) 5 shot down one of the escorting 'Zeroes'.

On the 26th, the Hellcats had their first partial success against the Kamikazes. Task Unit 77.4.1 was attacked by five D4Ys with four A6M5s as escort, and *Santee's* VF-26 beat off the first attempt at close range. However, the suicide pilots made a second approach and hit *Suwanee* again, this time inflicting major damage and heavy personnel casualties. *Sangamon* and *Petrof Bay* were both near-missed.

Halsey's fast carriers had been chasing the retreating Japanese Fleet during this day, and he was requested to return to provide support for the Leyte area. Task Force 38 had been in action for 17 days and the aircrew were becoming exhausted, while aircraft losses had not been completely made good by replacement. Two groups remained in the Leyte area for the next four days, with only six day carriers. On 28th October, TG 38.4 was in the process of striking at shipping off Cebu Island when forty-four Japanese aircraft made a conventional bombing attack; detected in time, the raid was broken up and thirteen shot down, but for the loss of four Hellcats – shorter odds than the Japanese had enjoyed for months. On the following day, the three carriers of TG 38.2 sent a sweep over the Manila area, where seventy-one Japanese aircraft were shot down for the loss of ten Hellcats. As the strike was returning, a Kamikaze slipped past the CAP and made the first successful attack on the fast carriers, inflicting slight damage on *Intrepid*.

TG 38.4 covered the Leyte area on 30th October, providing CAP and close support. During the afternoon, six Kamikazes from Cebu approached the group: short of CAP aircraft, and lacking accurate height information, the FDO assumed that the enemy were approaching at low-level for a pull-up attack and sent the Hellcats out at below 10,000 feet. The A6Ms were in fact at 18,000 feet and thus made their attack unopposed, except for AA fire. *Franklin* and *Belleau Wood* were both hit and badly damaged, 148 men being killed and forty-five aircraft destroyed by explosion and fire. TG. 38.4 was obliged to return to the forward base at Ulithi, leaving only TG 38.2, with two day carriers and *Independence* to act as distant cover for Leyte. Fortunately, the airfields on the island were just becoming operational, so that the USAAF could take the defensive task at least.

Task Force 38 returned to the Philippines on 5th November to attack the Japanese air forces, reinforced from Formosa and the Home Islands during the week's respite from carrier strikes. On this day and the next, over 400 Japanese aircraft were destroyed, mainly on the Luzon airfields, although the first sweep over Clark Field on 5th claimed to have destroyed fifty-eight Japanese fighters. On the same day, one of four Kamikaze A6Ms broke through the CAP and hit the Force flagship, *Lexington*, on the bridge, inflicting 182 casualties but failing to put her out of action.

Further strikes were delivered on 10th, 13th, 14th and 19th November, but not until the last did the Japanese manage to gather a small attack force which was turned back by CAP. On 25th November, however, after a break of six days, the enemy had sufficient aircraft to mount a determined raid. Task Groups 38.2 and .3 were within 100 miles of the Luzon coast at noon, when aircraft were detected less than 30 miles distant, approaching at high speed, in numbers too great to be plotted in the time available. A CAP division intercepted six A6Ms, but three of the Kamikazes got past and although no direct hits were scored, *Hancock* was hit by a blazing wing, shot off by AA fire. Twenty minutes later, twelve Kamikazes attacked TG 38.2 again, scoring two hits on *Intrepid* and a hit and a near-miss on *Cabot*. At the same time, *Essex*, in TG 38.3, was hit and lightly damaged. Only *Intrepid* had been put out of action, but the Japanese had clearly found the answer to the carriers' defences and operations by less than three groups were therefore suspended until counter-measures could be devised.

While Task Force 38 was at Ulithi during the latter part of November, the Staffs had been revising defensive tactics. To give longer warning of the

30th October, 1944: a 'Zero' dives out of the clouds onto *Franklin* to score a hit by the deck-edge elevator, in spite of numerous AA hits. (*USN 80-G-310038*)

approach of low-level raids, destroyers equipped with suitable radar would be deployed as 'pickets', up to 60 miles away from the carriers, in the direction of the most likely threat. 'Tomcat Pickets' would act as 'de-lousing' stations, with all returning strike aircraft passing within sight of them to ensure that no Japanese aircraft had tacked themselves on to get past the CAPS. The 'Tomcats' were to be provided with their own CAP, in order to deal with any gatecrashers. 'Jack Patrols' were also instituted as a regular feature – divisions of fighters at low level outside the destroyer screen and controlled visually by certain destroyers to provide a fast reaction last-ditch defence. Greater flexibility in the direction of aircraft was gained by an increased readiness of the Group FDOs to hand over the control of CAPs to those ships in the best position to handle the interceptions. The congested R/T channels became even more congested by the increase in size of the standing CAP and the number of controlling stations, by the system was limited by the number of VHF R/T transmitters which could be fitted in the ships (only about six in an *Essex*-class) and the mutual interference problems to which VHF radio transmitters were liable. The fighter was still the F6F-5 Hellcat, which lacked the acceleration and rate of climb to cope with close-range defence, but the number of fighters was to be increased from fifty-four (approved in September 1944) to seventy-three, at the expense of the dive-bomber squadrons, which were to be reduced to a strength of fifteen SB2Cs. When TF 38 went back to the firing line in December, two carriers, *Lexington* – VF-20 – and *Ticonderoga* – VF-80, had these enlarged fighter squadrons, but both were fresh from reserve and lacked experience.

The superiority of the Hellcat as an offensive fighter was put to the usual advantage over Luzon between 14th and 16th December 1944, while TF 38 supported the invasion of Mindoro. Commander J. S. Thach, now serving on the staff of Vice Admiral J. S. McCain, commanding the fast carriers, organised the sweeps so that Hellcats were overhead Japanese airfields during daylight hours, while night-fighters interdicted during the night.

This was the famous 'Big Blue Blanket' – 497 day fighters and thirty-nine night-fighters – which destroyed forty-six out of the sixty-nine Japanese aircraft which took off on 14th and thereafter prevented all organised movement on the airfields. VF-80 found twenty-seven A6Ms and Nakajima Ki 43 'Oscar' fighters attempting to fly in from Formosa, and the eight Hellcats destroyed twenty of the enemy at no cost to themselves. Total Japanese aircraft losses for the period were over 170 in the air and on the ground, for the loss of twenty-seven US Navy aircraft – many to AA fire. The escort carrier FM-2s defending the invasion force had destroyed a score of enemy aircraft, and the Kamikazes from the Central and Southern Philippines managed to sink only two Landing Ships (Tank) and damage four other ships during the period.

After a considerable battering in a typhoon on 18th December, Task Force 38 retired to Ulithi to prepare for the next major operation – the invasion of Luzon, at Lingayen Gulf. At Ulithi, the first US Marine Corps squadrons to see embarked service – VMF-124 and VMF-213 – joined *Essex*, bringing thirty-seven F4U-1D Corsairs to add to the fifty-four F6Fs of VF-4. The SB2Cs of VB-4 were landed and VT-4 was reduced to fifteen TBMs. Standard US Marine Corps fighter equipment since July 1943, the Corsair was now getting its first chance to see combat from an American carrier.

Royal Navy 1943-44 The Royal Navy had flown its first Corsair mission as long ago as 3rd April 1944, when two squadrons had provided top cover for a strike on the German battleship *Tirpitz*. In the same month, two other Corsair squadrons had joined US Navy Hellcats from *Saratoga* in an Anglo-American carrier strike on Sabang, Sumatra. The Corsair saw no action against the Luftwaffe in the course of half-a-dozen European operations, but in a return to Sabang on 25th July 1944, aircraft from *Illustrious* and *Victorious* splashed five A6M3s and a Mitsubishi Ki 21 'Sally' bomber, at no cost to themselves. Three operations later, in October, *Victorious's* 1834 Squadron became involved in a hectic dog-fight with nine Ki 43 'Oscars' over the Nicobar Islands and destroyed four and damaged the others, but at the cost of two Corsairs to the nimble, fast-climbing Japanese Army fighters. In raids on Sumatran oil targets in January 1945, the two carriers' Corsairs destroyed another fifteen Japanese fighters, for the loss of three Corsairs in air combat. Although these victories were few in number compared with the US Navy pilots' mammoth scores, it must be remembered that the British carriers had not yet undertaken extended operations in areas where the enemy possessed large numbers of aircraft and the only prolonged carrier operations had been off Salerno, in September 1943, and off the South of France, in August 1944.

For the former operation, four escort carriers and a 'Maintenance and Repair Carrier' – *Unicorn* – had been armed with 106 Seafires, which flew medium and low-level patrols over the Allied beach-head, turning back many Luftwaffe fighter-bomber raids but destroying only two Messerschmitt Bf 109s between 9th and 12th September. For the South of France invasion, seven Royal Navy escort carriers were joined by two US Navy CVEs. USS *Tulagi* and *Kasaan Bay* and HMS *Emperor* were armed with Hellcats, *Stalker*, *Hunter*, *Attacker* and *Khedive* with Seafires, and *Pursuer*

A Corsair II of 1836 Squadron on patrol over the Indian Ocean. The 'T' which identifies it as belonging to *Victorious* has been chalked in roughly. (*D. T. Chute*)

Five Squadrons of Hellcats operated from British escort carriers in the Bay of Bengal during 1945, striking at targets in Burma, Malaya and Sumatra and supporting several assault operations. This Hellcat I of *Khedive's* 809 Squadron is seen in flight over Ceylon. (*via W. B. Black*)

While the Marianas campaign was in progress, the Royal Navy escort carriers were preparing for the invasion of the South of France. Hellcats of 800 Squadron (*Emperor*) and Wildcat Vs (FM-1) of 882 Squadron (*Searcher*) overfly HMS *Pursuer*, with the Wildcat VIs of 881 Squadron on deck, during the work-up for the operation. (*IWM A25042*)

and *Searcher* with FM-1 Wildcat Vs and FM-2 Wildcat VIs respectively. British Hellcats had also gone into action for the first time on 3rd April, off the Norwegian coast, and had scored their first victories on 8th May, when four aircraft of 800 Squadron had been bounced by Focke-Wulf Fw 190A and Bf 109G fighters. One Hellcat had been shot down immediately, but the other three each destroyed a German aircraft. In the South of France operation, however, there were few enemy aircraft to be found and the only victories were scored by VF-74 (*Kasaan Bay*), which shot down three Junkers Ju 52/3 transports; the bulk of the carrier fighters' missions were spent interdicting German transport, spotting for ships' gun bombardments of the coast, and providing CAPs for the carrier force.

1

2

3

4

Cat in Hell – the
barrier has sliced
through the drop
tank suspension,
allowing the tank to
fly forward into the
propeller. The VF-9
(*Lexington*) pilot
escaped by jumping
off the wingtip. (*US
Navy 80-G-268188*)

142

Bombardment by naval fighter aircraft had first been tried on a large scale during the Normandy invasion, in June 1944. Four British squadrons, flying Seafires and Spitfires, had spotted for battleships and cruisers in the eastern sector, and a US Navy unit – VCS-7 – made up from the pilots of American battleship and cruiser spotter floatplanes, had been given *Spitfires* – the only US Navy unit to take the famous fighter into action!

The Royal Navy's first experience of suicide attack occurred on 29th January 1945, when the four armoured carriers *Victorious*, *Illustrious*, *Indomitable* and *Indefatigable* were recovering strike aircraft. Seven Japanese Army Ki 48 'Lily' bombers attacked at low level, undetected until they were within gun range – the low-level CAP was provided by the Seafires of 894 Squadron, and four pilots accounted for six bombers, sharing one with AA fire, one with a Corsair, and a third with a Hellcat which destroyed the seventh 'Lily' single-handed. The Seafire's phenomenal acceleration and speed into the turn had made this victory possible, for all but one of the interceptions had taken place within the destroyer screen. After this action, the British Pacific Fleet left the East Indies for Sydney, to prepare for operations with the US Pacific Fleet off Okinawa.

Lingayen Before the Okinawa operation, all available American carriers took part in the Lingayen campaign, seven large and five Light carriers for day operations, *Enterprise* and *Independence* with forty-eight F6F-5N and -5E Hellcats for night operations, and seventeen CVEs with 291 FM-2s for close-support and invasion force CAP. The Japanese had flown more reinforcements in during the carriers' break from operations, and over 500 were left on Luzon when the fast carriers returned. Poor weather prevented the 'Big Blue Blanket' from covering the island, but Task Force 38 flew 3,000 sorties between 3rd and 9th January 1945, one half of the number being sweeps and strikes against Luzon, Formosa and Okinawa. Twenty-two enemy aircraft were shot down, but forty-six American aircraft were lost in action and forty more (thirteen of them *Essex* Corsairs) lost in various accidents. Flak accounted for most of the combat losses, suffered in attacks on airfields, where less than 200 enemy aircraft were destroyed or damaged.

Task Force 38 thus failed to eliminate the threat, and the Kamikazes struck hard at the invasion force – Task Force 77. Between 3rd January and 'S-Day' (9th January), less than 100 Kamikazes took off to attack, escorted by about forty fighters: between them, they scored thirty-four hits or damaging near-misses on twenty-nine ships, sinking the escort carrier *Ommaney Bay* and a destroyer, and damaging the escort carriers *Savo Is*, *Manila Bay*, *Kadashan Bay* and *Kitkun Bay*, the last two being forced to return to Leyte. The FM-2 CAP, twenty-four strong, managed to break up two attacks on 5th January, destroying a dozen A6Ms and D3As, but on the following day the fighters were unable to check the Kamikazes, twelve out of twenty-eight scoring hits. The escort carriers and fighter direction ships were less than 50 miles off-shore and the radar returns from the coast and the vast number of ships made detection of raids difficult, but the main causes were the lack of experience of the FDOs, the less comprehensive radar equipment of the CVEs and HQ ships, and the poor performance of the FM-2 compared with the A6M5 Kamikazes and their escorts.

After the landings in Lingayen Gulf, the Kamikazes hit eleven more

Opposite.

1.
A 'Zeke 52' turns tight to shake off a pursuing Wildcat over the Philippines (*USN 80-9 183909*)

2.
Lieutenant D. S. Ogle, flying a Seafire LRIIC of 809 Squadron (*Stalker*), set this Junkers Ju 88 on fire near Athens and then took photographs of the subsequent crash with the port-facing reconnaissance still camera.

3.
The British carriers met their first suicide aircraft on 29th January, 1945, off Sumatra. Here *Victorious* steams between the burning wreckage of two Ki 48 'Lily' bombers shot down by Seafires.

4.
When *Essex* returned to sea on 30th December, 1944, she was carrying the 36 Marine Corps Corsairs of VMF-124 and -213, as well as the 54 Hellcats of VF-4. Here, a running range of fighters prepares to take-off during operations in the South China Sea. (*US Navy*)

143

ships up to 13th January, when the CVE *Salamaua* was severely damaged. In spite of their limitations, the Wildcats had shot down over sixty aircraft around the force – it is almost certain, however, that some of the claims included aircraft which subsequently crashed into ships or into the water at the end of an attack, making it difficult to apportion the responsibility for the splash.

Task Force 38 spent the days between 9th and 20th January in an anti-shipping offensive in the China Sea. Relatively few enemy aircraft were destroyed, but the Marine Corsair squadrons claimed ten in the air, Lieutenant W. McGill of VMF-124 destroying three A6Ms in three minutes on 20th.

Formosa was attacked on 21st January. The fast carriers had not come under attack during the operation so far, and the defensive organisation was relaxed when four Kamikazes struck at noon. *Langley* was hit by a bomb and put out of action for three hours, but *Ticonderoga* received heavy damage when an A6M crashed into her crowded deck, starting widespread fires. Forty minutes later she was hit again, by the sole survivor of a group of eight Kamikazes, and the carrier had to be withdrawn to Ulithi, having sustained 345 casualties. The 'Tomcat' picket destroyers were attacked soon afterwards by a suicide aircraft which had followed a strike home: *Maddox* was hit but suffered only 'moderate' damage. A prime cause of this wave of successful attacks was the bad R/T discipline of many of the fighter pilots, who indulged in unnecessary chatter which blocked the FDOs' instructions to the CAPs. The veteran VF-22 from *Cowpens* achieved the only completely successful interception of the day, eight Hellcats shooting down or driving off seven Kamikazes and six fighters – Luzon's last remaining suicide formation.

The Fast Carrier Task Force spent 25th January to 10th February at Ulithi. By the time that damaged carriers had left for the US and new and repaired ships had joined, the redesignated TF 58 possessed nine large and five Light carriers for day operations and *Enterprise* and *Saratoga* for night work. Six more Marine Corsair squadrons embarked, two aboard each of *Bennington*, *Wasp* and *Bunker Hill*, and most of the other large carriers had increased the size of their fighter squadrons from fifty-four to seventy-three Hellcats.

Iwo Jima On 16th February, the Hellcats and Corsairs took the war to the heart of the Japanese Empire, sweeping over the Tokyo area airfields. The bad weather over Japan hampered the sweeps, but enemy fighters were encountered in large numbers. Although over 300 were claimed as shot down, it was at the highest cost for many months, sixty American aircraft being lost in combat. The newer air groups suffered hardest, for lacking experience the young pilots attempted to dog-fight with the more manoeuvrable A6Ms and N1K1-J 'Georges', flown by some of the more experienced pilots left to the Japanese Navy. The eight Marine Corps squadrons destroyed eleven aircraft, but lost ten Corsairs, some of these due to the navigational inexperience of their pilots.

Iwo Jima was invaded on 19th February 1945, with close support provided by TF 58 and escort carriers. After D-Day, the fast carriers moved away to provide distant support, striking at the Bonin Islands as well as flying scheduled attacks on the Iwo Jima defences. *Saratoga* was detached to join the escort carriers in order to give night cover, but on 21st February she was hit by five Kamikazes out of six which had attacked. The carrier had detected the raid at long range, but the Air Support Commander in the HQ ship *Estes* – solely responsible for aircraft movements within the Iwo Jima area – evaluated the contact as 'friendly'; nevertheless, six day-fighter Hellcats of VF(N)-53 were vectored out and found eight decidedly unfriendly 'Zeroes', two of which were promptly shot down. The others evaded into cloud, and although *Saratoga* managed to scramble fifteen F6F-5Ns in the 10 minutes which elapsed before the first Kamikaze attacked, the fighters were unable to reach an intercepting position.

Another five Kamikazes attacked after dusk, and one of these scored yet another hit. Badly damaged, *Saratoga* withdrew to Eniwetok and then the US for repairs – she was used only for training thereafter.

At the same time that *Saratoga* was hit for the sixth time, G4M 'Betties' made a torpedo/suicide attack on another CVE group, sinking *Bismarck Sea* and damaging *Lunga Point*. No night-fighters had been available, owing to the attacks on the night carrier. *Enterprise* took *Saratoga*'s place on 22nd February and remained as part of TG 52.2 until 10th March, her Avengers and Hellcats flying 174 consecutive hours from 23rd February to 2nd March. Half-a-dozen enemy aircraft were shot down by the night-fighters from 'the world's biggest Jeep carrier – *Enterprise Bay*'.

The lack of night-fighters in escort carriers was partly solved by the deployment of VF(N)-33 aboard *Sangamon* in March 1945. In February 1945, the US Marine Corps was given the first of four escort carriers – *Block Island*: although the F4U-1D was the preferred day-fighter, VMF-511 also operated ten Hellcats, eight -5Ns and two photo-reconnaissance -5Ps. *Gilbert Islands* followed three months later, with *Cape Gloucester* and *Vella Gulf* joining by early June, all armed in a similar fashion to *Block Island*.

'Iceberg' The next target for invasion on the United States' list was Okinawa, between Japan and Formosa. The campaign lasted nearly three months, from 26th March to 22nd June 1945, and during that period no fewer than forty-four American and seven British carriers took part in Operation 'Iceberg'. Twenty-one American and five of the British carriers were the fast ships of Task Forces 58 and 57 (British Pacific Fleet), in covering positions to the north-east and south-west of Okinawa, while the CVEs supported the US Army and Marines on the island, provided CAP over the anchorages, hunted for submarines, and interdicted airfields on other islands in the Ryukyu chain.

For an island so close to Japan itself – less than 300 miles – the enemy could be expected to react very strongly. US Navy intelligence estimates gave the Japanese barely 3,000 aircraft with which suicide attacks could be mounted. In fact, by dint of giving pilots the bare minimum of training needed for their one-way trip, the Japanese could count on nearly double that number, of which 2,000 were ear-marked for Kamikaze use at the beginning of April. The considerable experience gained in Kamikaze tactics since October 1944 enabled more formalised attacks to be made, with radar-fitted shadowers reporting the positions of targets and radar-fitted navigational shepherds leading the suicide aircraft to the target. Radar and flares made night attacks possible, although it was hoped that conventional torpedo attacks would also prove to be fruitful.

Against this threat, the American and British Navies could deploy over 1,300 fighters. Of these, 580 were day Hellcats, ninety-two night-fighter Hellcats (including sixteen aboard *Sangamon*), 380 Corsairs, 280 Wildcats, forty Seafires and twelve Fireflies. The Corsair had been embarked in quantity for this operation, with six of the ten large day carriers operating either Marine Corps squadrons or US Navy VBF (fighter-bomber) squadrons equipped with F4U-1Ds or cannon-armed -1Cs (VF-10 and VBF-10 aboard *Intrepid*). Two British carriers also had Corsairs – F4U-1Bs – and when *Illustrious* was relieved by *Formidable* in mid-April, the latter was also carrying Corsairs, in her case F4U-1Ds and the Goodyear-built FG-1Ds. HMS *Indomitable* was alone in the Royal Navy in carrying Hellcats (although several escort carriers were so armed), but her No 5 Fighter Wing was to build up an enviable reputation as an all-round general-purpose fighter unit. *Indefatigable's* forty Seafires were in many ways a liability, for their poor deck-landing characteristics were the cause of most of the losses of this type, and their short endurance prevented their offensive use. There was also a shortage of divisional leaders in the Seafire Wing, although many of the young pilots had served in the two squadrons for nearly a year and had seen more combat than their counterparts in the Royal Navy Corsair and Hellcat units. The Fireflies were of little use defensively, and their main role was to be flak suppression for the Avenger strikes on the airfields of the Sakishima Gunto.

Extensive use was made of the picket destroyer system off Okinawa, particularly to give advanced warning of the approach of aircraft from Kyushu towards the transport anchorage. Sixteen stations, at up to 75 miles from the invasion beaches, were designated, but of these only twelve were ever filled, and on 'L-Day' (1st April 1945) only eight were occupied, with nineteen suitably-equipped destroyers available. CAPs were provided for the pickets by TF 58 and the CVEs of TG 52.1, but the main fighter direction task was to be undertaken by six HQ ships, of which only three were fitted and manned for night-fighter control. Many ships carried visual FDOs, but American faith in the 'Jack' patrols was not complete.

The Royal Navy, on the other hand, had given a convincing demonstration of low-level close-range air defences off Sumatra in January, and was to rely upon a division of Seafires at low level, another division of Seafires and one of Hellcats or Corsairs at medium level, and a division of Corsairs at high level. More aircraft would be held at readiness on deck. With 100 fewer fighters than the average Group of TF 58, the British Pacific Fleet could not afford to maintain eight divisions on CAP, in addition to the escort and TARCAP commitment. One advantage was of course the smaller number of radar contacts permanently around the force, but the British pilots' R/T discipline was undoubtedly better than that of the Americans, and after an extra two years of war, the British fighter direction system had maintained its superiority. The Royal Navy FDOs had been trained to handle three radar interceptions at one time (and had done so in the Mediterranean) and IFF operating technique had been drummed into pilots

and direction officers alike, so that the radar displays were less liable to be swamped with the wide IFF signals than was the case with TF 58. The one lack in TF 57 was that of a night-fighter: a few Hellcat pilots had been 'night-qualified' – they could take off and land in the dark – but there were no radar-equipped aircraft for them. British ship radar was generally good, with better high-altitude and low cover than the American sets, but lacking their very long-range detection capabilities.

A would-be Kamikaze burns on the water as Task Force 58 operates in support of the Okinawa invasion. (*US Navy*)

The first Kamikazes struck even before Task Force 58 left Ulithi. Twenty-four P1Y 'Frances' bombers made a 1,400-mile one-way trip from Kanoya and although half returned due to various malfunctions, twelve of the others got through to the area of the anchorage during the night of 11th/12th March. Two hits were scored – one on an islet mistaken for a carrier, and the other on *Randolph*, lit-up while taking on ammunition. She missed the first fortnight of operations, but the repairs were carried out in a forward area.

TF 58 struck at Kyushu, Shikoku and southern Honshu on 18th and 19th March. Fighter sweeps on the first day met few Japanese fighters, but the CAP was fully engaged with Kamikazes and conventional attack aircraft. *Enterprise*, *Intrepid* and *Yorktown* were all slightly damaged by aircraft which broke through the CAP, and over thirty were destroyed by the defending fighters and AA fire. On 19th March the carrier aircraft concentrated on warships at Kure and Kobe, but the Japanese bombers found and attacked TG 58.2 as the latter was about to launch a second strike. Five 'Judies' from Kanoya made a completely undetected attack scoring direct bomb hits on *Franklin* and *Wasp*, but failing to inflict suicide damage. Both carriers were very severely damaged – *Franklin* was not repaired before the end of the war – and 825 of the ships' companies were killed and 534 injured by the explosions and fires.

The carriers began to withdraw, covering the damaged ships, and it was not until the afternoon of the next day that an attack by eighteen aircraft was detected. Three were turned away by the CAP, which shot down seven others, but the remainder broke through again, although the carriers had over 100 fighters in the air. Seven more A6Ms were shot down by AA fire, and the sole survivor overshot *Hancock* but hit the destroyer which had been refuelling from the carrier. The force was shadowed during the night, in spite of a couple of successes by *Enterprise*'s night-fighters, and four raids were despatched by the Japanese. Only one was able to find TF 58, but detected at long range it was first intercepted by twenty-four Corsairs and Hellcats from TG 58.1; all serviceable carriers scrambled more fighters, until over 150 were in the air. The raid consisted of eighteen G4M2E 'Betty' bombers, each carrying an MXY-8 'Okha' piloted rocket-bomb (code-named 'Baka' by the Allies), and escorted by thirty A6M5s. While the Corsairs held off the escort, the Hellcats of VF-30 (*Belleau Wood*) and VF and VBF-17 (*Hornet*) destroyed all the G4Ms and their unlaunched suicide missiles; the 'Zekes' could do little to help the bombers, and about twenty of them were destroyed, for the sole loss of a VBF-17 Hellcat. In a straight-forward medium-level interception such as this, the US Navy fighter pilots and their direction officers were superb.

The Okinawa campaign opened on 25th March, when amphibious forces arrived off the Kerama Retto, a small group of islands within 20 miles of Okinawa which were to be occupied as a forward base and ancho-rage. Small numbers of Kamikazes from Kyushu and Formosa got through and damaged eleven ships during the following week, when the main re-sponsibility for air defence rested with single Groups of TF 58. Task Force 57 began operations on 26th March but encountered no air opposition until 1st April, the day of the landings on Okinawa itself.

Four ships were hit during dawn and twilight attacks on the assaulting forces, but the only attack on carriers was delivered against the British ships off Sakishima Gunto. Three A6Ms broke through the Hellcat and Corsair CAP and the first was seen at about 3,000 feet over the carriers by Sub Lieutenant R. H. Reynolds, flying a 'Jack' patrol Seafire of 894 Squadron. Reynolds managed to close this aircraft and score hits on it, but the A6M pulled through and dived on *Indefatigable*, crashing at the base of the island but inflicting little damage on the 3-inch armour. Another A6M was seen and chased – this one dropped a bomb which near-missed and damaged a screening destroyer before the Seafire could catch it and destroy it just outside the screen. Reynolds then saw the third A6M, which tried to get away, and then, when overtaken, tried to out-manoeuvre the Seafire. Fighting on the climb and dive, Reynolds was consistently able to cut across the tighter turn of the 'Zero' and eventually destroyed it with the last of his ammunition. This fairly typical Royal Navy pilot served for 13 months in 894 Squadron but saw enemy aircraft on only three occasions – once off Norway, when he shared in the destruction of two shadowers, the combat described, and another on 4th May, when he shared an A6M. Had he been given the opportunity for more frequent combat, there can be little doubt that he, like many other British pilots, would have been able to run up a high score, instead of the $3\frac{1}{2}$ victories which made him the top-scoring Seafire pilot.

The Japanese continued to make small-scale suicide attacks up to 5th April, but on the following day they launched 355 Kamikaze sorties and 341 bomber and escort sorties, all but three against the Okinawa area. Poor weather during the forenoon meant that the raids were concentrated into a four-hour period, between 1400 and 1800. Task Force 58 was attack-

On 12th April, 1945, a pair of 1770 Squadron Fireflies met five Mitsubishi Ki 51 'Sonia' light bombers off Formosa and destroyed four and damaged the fifth. (*via G. E. Pugh*)

The crews of the Fireflies, left to right: Lieutenant R. H. Ward, Sub Lieutenant P. Stott (pilot), Sub Lieutenant E. Miller, Lieutenant W. Thomson. (*FAA Museum*)

'Baka'-carrying Betties fall to *Hornet* Hellcats – 21 March 1945 (*US Navy*)

Above.

Another near-miss: A P1Y1 'Frances' leaves a fiery trail over the stern of an escort carrier off Okinawa. (*USN*)

Below left.

The war in Europe ended during the Okinawa campaign: HMS *Queen*'s 853 Squadron was one of the last British units to fire a shot in anger, her Wildcat VIs chasing a Ju 88 away from an occupation convoy bound for Denmark, on 8th May. The out-rigger stowages enabled aircraft to be landed on while fighters remained at readiness for take-off. (*Mod(N)*)

ed by large numbers, but these Kamikazes were not as effective as their predecessors, and over fifty were shot down by CAP, while those which got through near-missed three carriers, two cruisers, and two destroyers. The fast carriers were also reinforcing the CAP over the picket destroyers and the Okinawa area. The Wildcats, Hellcats and Corsairs were faced with more targets than they could shoot down in the time, a division of VF-9 (*Yorktown*) Hellcats *claiming* to have shot down fifty Japanese between them! Setting aside such inflated claims, it would appear that the CVE Wildcats destroyed fifty-five aircraft, TF 58 aircraft about 100, and AA fire thirty-five. In spite of all the efforts of the defence, thirty-nine Kamikazes scored direct hits or damaging near-misses, sinking six ships and damaging fourteen others; four other ships were damaged by 'normal' bombing.

This 'Kikusui' mass suicide attack was the heaviest sent in by the Japanese. There were three more during April, the strongest of which included 185 Kamikazes, including a few 'Bakas', with just under 200 other bombers and fighters. On this day, 12th April, the defences claimed 208 Japanese aircraft shot down, but twenty-four ships were hit, two being sunk.

In spite of all the experience of fighting Kamikazes, the British and American forces never really got the measure of the suicide aircraft. Between 26th March and 22nd June, 1,900 Japanese Navy and Army Kamikazes attacked, sinking twenty-six ships and damaging 176 others, some of the latter on several occasions. During the same period, the enemy lost 2,200 conventional bombers and fighters in the process of sinking two ships and damaging sixty-one – a startling indication of the relative effectiveness of suicide attack. Five American and four British carriers were hit, on twelve separate occasions – *Enterprise* was hit three times and HMS *Formidable* twice, and two American CVEs were hit. None was sunk, and the armoured British carriers did not even have to withdraw for repairs.

The radar picket destroyers, which were to give early warning of raids, were themselves the targets of intensive attacks, by up to thirty aircraft at a time, and of thirty-three ships used on this duty, six were sunk, thirteen seriously damaged, and five slightly damaged. Landing craft plentifully armed with close-range AA guns were posted in support of the destroyers, and these too suffered, four being sunk and eight damaged by Kamikazes. No fewer than fourteen of the thirty-six casualties occurred on Station One, 50 miles north of the anchorage, where an almost permanent daylight CAP was maintained; over 300 Kamikazes were drawn to this one station during April. The anti-submarine pickets, inside the radar warning line, also drew more than their fair share of the Kamikazes, two being sunk and thirty-one damaged.

The claims for the destruction of enemy aircraft were very high. Task Force 58, which became TF 38 again on 28th May, claimed to have destroyed 1,266 enemy aircraft, over 750 of which were modern fighters, for the loss of only *ten* fighters in combat. Ninety of the victories were scored by the night-fighter Hellcats, whose task had been harder than ever due to the strict gun-fire zone restrictions as much as to the evasive manoeuvres of the targets; many promising chases, with the fighter in firm contact, had to be broken off to remain clear of the gun zones.

The Hellcats and Wildcats of TG 52.1 destroyed 126 enemy aircraft

Opposite right.

Bunker Hill was put out of the war on 11th May, 1945, when she was hit by a suicide 'Zero' and then a 554 lb bomb dropped by a 'Judy'. Four other Kamikazes were shot down by VMF-221 and VMF-451, bringing their score for four months' operations to 84 enemy aircraft destroyed. 404 men died and 256 were injured in the fires which burned for five hours. (*USN 80-G-323712*)

around Okinawa, at a cost of only one fighter of each type. During 1944, the Wildcat had enjoyed the best kill:loss ratio in the US Navy, and the Okinawa campaign, in which the loss rate was 1:80, maintained the US Navy's faith in this wonderful little fighter.

The Royal Navy's carrier pilots had not met such heavy opposition, but forty-two enemy aircraft had been destroyed, eight by Seafires, four by Fireflies, and the remainder by the Hellcats and Corsairs. No British fighter had been shot down in air combat, although two had been lost to the carriers' own AA guns while chasing Kamikazes through the gun defence zone.

The Home Islands The final operations against Japan were almost an anti-climax. On 10th July 1945, TF 38's eight large and six Light carriers began striking at the Home Islands. Joined later in the month by two more large carriers, and four British Fleet carriers, the shipboard aircraft ranged the length and breadth of Japan until 13th August, interrupted only by the need to replenish the ships, typhoons, and the two atomic bomb attacks on 6th and 9th August. The Japanese made little attempt to interfere with the strikes as they were husbanding their remaining air strength for the inevitable invasion. It is worth noting, however, that the last non-nuclear Boeing B-29 raid, on Sawata, was intercepted by over 100 Army and Navy fighters on 8th August: no carrier strike was accorded this welcome – the Japanese knew too well that waves of fighters would follow any interceptors back to their bases and wipe them out on the ground. Apart from a single attempt at a dusk torpedo attack on 25th July, when F6F-5Ns from *Bonhomme Richard's* VF(N)-91 destroyed six Aichi B7A 'Graces' and two radarless Hellcat IIs of *Formidable's* 1844 Squadron destroyed another three, the first attack on TF 38 occurred after the Nagasaki bomb. During the afternoon of 9th August, the destroyer *Borie*, on picket duty 50 miles from the carriers, was Kamikazed by a D3A 'Val' – the latter thus gaining the honour of delivering the last successful suicide attack and the former achieving the doubtful honour of being the last victim, although she was not sunk.

Japanese aircraft attempted to strike TF 38 on 12th August, but eighteen would-be Kamikazes were shot down by the CAP, Task Group 38.3's being controlled by HMS *Indefatigable* to destroy five of the enemy. This ship's Seafires were also involved in the last British air combat of the war: ten Seafires of 887 and 894 Squadrons were escorting Avengers of 820 Squadron over Odaki Bay on 15th August when twelve A6M5s attacked. Eight of the 'Zekes' were shot down by the Seafires and one by the Avengers, for the loss of a British aircraft of each type. The American strikes also met airborne opposition, between thirty and forty Japanese aircraft being shot down over the Tokyo area. The last combat fell to *Yorktown's* VF-88, part of an air group which had joined the carrier since the Okinawa campaign. Bounced by a dozen A6Ms, the six Hellcats fought back, claiming to have destroyed nine of their assailants but only two Hellcats returned.

The cease-fire prevented a second strike on this day, but individual Japanese aircraft attempted to make Kamikaze attacks on TF 38 up to 1100. The last fell within 100 yards of *Indefatigable*, shot down by Corsairs from *Shangri-La* (VF-85).

Independence, operating as a 'day carrier' again, rolls in the heavy swell off Japan during the final strikes. The two VF-27 Hellcats are positioned on the catapults, ready to 'Scramble'. (*US Navy*)

Left.
More co-operation with *Essex:* a *Victorious* Corsair taxies up the American wooden deck, the British pilot having responded appropriately to the rather different landing signals. (*US Navy*)

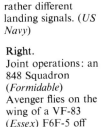

Right.
Joint operations: an 848 Squadron (*Formidable*) Avenger flies on the wing of a VF-83 (*Essex*) F6F-5 off Japan. (*FAA Museum*)

The Seafires of 801 and 880 Squadrons saw no air combat during their service aboard *Implacable* in the last three months of the war, but they were used extensively for ground attack missions. To increase their radius of action, 89-Imperial-gallon fuel tanks designed for use on Curtiss P-40s were "borrowed' and adapted to the Seafire. (*M. Crosley*

The war with Japan had been brought to a sudden end by the dropping of the atomic bombs, but these had only been the final nails in a well-furnished coffin. Japan had been brought to her economic knees in January 1945, when the occupation of the east coast of Luzon had sealed her off from the oil and rice fields in the East Indies and Indo-China. Intensive minelaying of coastal waters by B-29s had strangled trade routes around the Home Islands, and the depredations of the American submarines had reduced Japan's shipping capacity to below the minimum tonnage needed to sustain an island economy. The carriers' part in the victory had been to clear the way for the island invasions which deprived the Japanese of defensive bases and gave the Americans offensive bases on an ever-contracting perimeter around the Empire. It was significant that the A-bomb B-29s had taken off from Tinian in the Marianas, for it was at the outset of the campaign that saw the capture of the island that the Hellcat had carved its name on the honours board, at the Battle of the Philippine Sea.

The United States Navy's aircraft won their ascendancy by seeking out the enemy in his own air space in all the later major battles. Doctrine had not been established until after the 1942 carrier battles, and not until the ships and aircraft became available in 1943 could the new concept of the offensive task force be developed as a strategy which would be one of the pillars of victory.

The Royal Navy's carriers' major contributions to the defeat of Germany were all made during the first half of the war, when the enemy held complete air superiority. The British carrier fighter pilots were thus on the defensive until the autumn of 1942, flying out-performed aircraft but developing the tactics for Fleet defence which would be used with only minor modifications to the end of the war. It would not be an exaggeration to state that Malta owed its survival to the aircraft carrier, just as Guadalcanal was held and cleared of Japanese thanks to the US Pacific Fleet carriers. The loss of either island in 1942 would have had the effect of prolonging the war still further, but both were saved by the availability of fully mobile air power.

The Japanese, who had started the war with such an excellent Fleet fighter, lost the initiative due to technical deficiencies. The lack of radar at Midway was followed by the failure to provide an aircraft which could regain the lost superiority. Those aircraft that there were, were thrown away by commitment to battle from shore bases, and there was never sufficient time to train new pilots once the American machine had gathered momentum, using the example of the Japanese carriers' exploits during the first six months of the Pacific War to roll back the Empire.

American Fleet fighters – the Grumman F4F and F6F, General Motors FM, and Vought F4U – destroyed 6,477 aircraft in air combat, according to a 1948 Office of Naval Intelligence press release. Of this total, 3,300 were claimed in 1944 alone. The Hellcat was credited with 4,947 victories at sea, as well as 209 from shore-bases; this immortal fighter was the most successful Allied aircraft of the war in air combat, even without the addition of the Royal Navy's thirty-seven victories with the type.

The Royal Navy's claims came to a modest 400 destroyed and 130 damaged, of which fifty were believed to have been 'probably destroyed'. The Fulmar was the most successful fighter, scoring 112 kills and damaging sixty-six enemy aircraft between 1st September 1940 and 2nd September 1942; next came the Martlet (renamed Wildcat in January 1944), which destroyed at least sixty-five aircraft.

By August 1945, the carriers were armed with fighters as good as any in the world, backed by a defensive system which had gained experience against every anticipated form of air attack, and against one which had never been foreseen. The umbrella over the Fleet might not have been watertight, but it kept out more of the enemy than any land-based equivalent during the war.

Appendix 1. Shipboard Fighters 1937–1945.

Note
symbols:
† denotes endurance with normal external fuel
‡ denotes endurance with maximum external fuel
§ denotes two-seat fighter

Aircraft	Manufacturer	Service	Period	Max Speed (mph/feet)	Ceiling (feet)	Endurance	Armament	Weight (lb)	Power (hp)
D 373/376	Dewoitine	France	1936–39	250 @ 13,000	32,800	1½ hours	4 × 7.5 mm	4,350	930
A5M 'Claude'	Mitsubishi	IJN	1937–41	273 @ 10,000	32,000	2½ hours	2 × 0.303 in	3,550	610
F3F-2	Grumman	USN	1938–41	256 @ 15,000	32,500	4 hours	1 × 0.3 in 1 × 0.5 in	4,450	950
§Skua	Blackburn	RN	1938–41	225 @ 6,500	18,200	4½ hours	5 × 0.303 in	8,230	905
Sea Gladiator	Gloster	RN	1939–40	245 @ 15,000	32,000	1½ hours	4 × 0.303 in	5,420	840
F3F-3	Grumman	USN	1939–41	261 @ 15,200	33,200	4 hours	2 × 0.303 in	4,615	950
F2A-1	Brewster	USN	1939–40	301 @ 17,000	32,500	4 hours	2 × 0.5 in	5,055	1,000
A6M2 'Zero'	Mitsubishi	IJN	1940–44	332 @ 15,000	32,800	6 hours	2 × 20 mm 2 × 7.7 mm	6,160	940
F2A-3	Brewster	USN	1941	321 @ 16,500	33,000	3½ hours	4 × 0.5 in	6,840	1,200
F4F-3	Grumman	USN	1941–42	310 @ 14,000	37,000	3½ hours	4 × 0.5 in	7,350	1,200
§Roc	Blackburn	RN	1939–40	219 @ 6,500	16,000	4 hours	4 × 0.303 in	8,800	905
§Fulmar I	Fairey	RN	1940–42	230 @ SL 247 @ 9,000	16,000	4 hours	8 × 0.303 in	10,700	1,080
Sea Hurricane IB	Hawker	RN	1941–42	315 @ 7,500 308 @ 18,000	32,000	1½ hours	8 × 0.303 in	7,015	1,030
Martlet II	Grumman	RN	1941–43	292 @ 6,000 300 @ 14,000	29,000	3 hours	6 × 0.5 in	7,747	1,200
§Fulmar II	Fairey	RN	1941–43	238 @ SL 259 @ 9,000	18,000	4 hours	8 × 0.303 in	10,350	1,300

Aircraft	Manufacturer	Service	Year	Speed @ altitude	Ceiling	Endurance	Armament	Weight	Range
F4F-4 Wildcat	Grumman	USN	1942–43	275 @ SL, 318 @ 19,500	35,000	3 hours	6 × 0.5 in	7,952	1,200
Seafire IIC	Supermarine	RN	1942–44	285 @ SL, 332 @ 14,000	28,000	1½ hours†	2 × 20 mm, 4 × 0.303 in	7,288	1,515
A6M3 'Hamp'	Mitsubishi	IJN	1942–44	288 @ SL, 315 @ 14,000, 335 @ 19,000	30,000	6 hours†	2 × 20 mm, 2 × 0.303 in	5,906	1,100
Seafire LIIC	Supermarine	RN	1943–44	316 @ SL, 338 @ 5,000	22,000	1½ hours†	2 × 20 mm etc	7,410	1,640
FM-1 Wildcat	Grumman/General Motors	USN RN	1943–45	292 @ 3,500, 313 @ 13,000	32,500	3 hours	4 × 0.5 in	7,811	1,200
Martlet IV	Grumman	RN	1942–44	286 @ 4,000, 296 @ 15,000	29,000	3 hours	6 × 0.5 in	7,730	1,240
F6F-3 Hellcat	Grumman	USN RN	1943–45	325 @ 3,000, 362 @ 18,500	35,500	3 hours†	6 × 0.5 in	12,365	2,000
Seafire FIII	Supermarine	RN	1944–45	304 @ SL, 352 @ 12,500	34,000	1½ hours†	2 × 20 mm etc	7,508	1,470
§Firefly I	Fairey	RN	1944–50	296 @ 3,500, 319 @ 7,000	28,500	3 hours	4 × 20 mm	12,131	1,735
A6M5 'Zeke 52'	Mitsubishi	IJN	1944	297 @ SL, 348 @ 20,000	36,500	5 hours†	2 × 20 mm, 2 × 0.303 in	6,025	1,100
Corsair II	Chance-Vought	RN	1944–45	357 @ 2,500, 397 @ 15,000	35,000	3 hours†	6 × 0.5 in	12,108	2,250
FM-2 Wildcat	Grumman/GM	USN RN	1944–45	307 @ 3,500, 328 @ 12,800	32,000	4 hours†	4 × 0.5 in	7,413	1,300
F6F-5 Hellcat	Grumman	USN RN	1944–45	340 @ 1,500, 380 @ 14,500, 407 @ 23,000	35,000	4 hours†	6 × 0.5 in	13,717	2,250
Seafire LIII	Supermarine	RN	1944–46	356 @ 6,000, 345 @ 12,500	25,000	3 hours‡	2 × 20 mm etc	7,750	1,585
F4U-1D Corsair (FG-1D)	Chance-Vought (Goodyear)	USN RN USMC	1945	362 @ 2,500, 406 @ 15,000, 415 @ 19,500	35,000	4 hours†	6 × 0.5 in	12,300	2,250

Three Allied fighter aircraft entered service after the end of hostilities. Their principal data are compared with those of the fighter which had been intended to replace the A6M in IJN service.

Type	Maker	Service	Dates	Speed	Armament	Ceiling	Endurance	Weight	Range
F8F-1 Bearcat	Grumman	USN	1945–50	394 @ SL / 434 @ 19,800	4 × 0.5 in	38,500	3½ hours	9,335	2,700
Seafire XV	Supermarine	RN / RCN	1945–48	369 @ 5,000 / 384 @ 13,500	2 × 20 mm etc	36,000	2 hours†	7,960	1,830
A7M 'Sam'	Mitsubishi	IJN	—	390 @ 21,500	2 × 20 mm	35,800	2 hours	10,400	2,200
F4U-4 Corsair	Chance-Vought	USN / USMC	1945–53	373 @ SL	6 × 0.5 in†	40,000	4½ hours†	13,550	2,700

Appendix 2. The Opposition 1939–1945.

Aircraft included in this list were those commonly encountered by Allied carrier fighters. The majority were reconnaissance and bomber types; in the case of the Japanese aircraft, these and others were frequently used as suicide attack aircraft.

The Role of the aircraft is denoted by a simple letter code: D = dive-bomber; FB = Fighter-bomber; L = Level bomber; MF = multi-seat fighter; R = Reconnaissance/Shadower; SF = single-seat fighter; T = Torpedo-bomber.

Speed is given in miles per hour at appropriate heights (SL = sea-level). In the case of certain Japanese aircraft – indicated by an asterisk (*) – the speeds are those obtained during flight tests of captured aircraft by pilots of the Technical Air Intelligence Centre, Anacostia. As these are often considerably in excess of the normally quoted figures, the latter are also provided, in parentheses.

Range is the maximum straight-line still air distance attainable, and is only an indication of the potential radius of action or endurance. Radius of Action is a practical figure and here denotes the reconnaissance aircraft's usual limit of range from base with a useful patrol time at that distance; for strike and bomber aircraft it denotes the weapons-carrying striking range; for escort fighters it denotes the range to which the bombers can be escorted. All distances are in statute miles (1,760 yards = 1.61 km).

German Aircraft

Type	Role	Speed	Range	Radius of Action	Ordnance Load (maximum)	Armament
Blohm & Voss Bv 138C	R	175 @ SL	2,700	800		1 × 7.92 mm / 1 × 13 mm / 2 × 20 mm
Dornier Do 18G	R	156 @ SL	2,175	500		1 × 13 mm / 1 × 20 mm

Aircraft		Speed			Bomb/torpedo load	Armament
Focke-Wulf Fw 200C	R/L	190 @ SL 224 @ 16,000	2,200	800	4,626 lb bombs or 2 × Hs 293 missiles	2 × 7.92 mm 3 × 13 mm 1 × 20 mm
Heinkel He 111P	L/T	225 @ SL (176 fully loaded) 247 @ 16,400 (200 fully loaded)	1,500	400	4,408 lb bombs or 2 torpedoes	6 × 7.92 mm
Heinkel He 115	R/T	186 @ SL 203 @ 11,000	2,080	400	1 torpedo	2 × 7.92 mm 1 × 20 mm
Junkers Ju 87R	D	210 @ SL 235 @ 13,500	600	200	1,102 lb bomb	2 × 7.92 mm (fixed) 1 × 7.92-mm (flexible)
Junkers Ju 88A	L/D/T/R	270 @ SL (War Emergency) 292 @ 17,500 (Combat Power)	1,700	400	4,408 lb bombs or 2 torpedoes	7 × 7.92 mm or 3 × 7.92 mm 2 × 13 mm
Messerschmitt Bf 109F	SF	330 @ SL 390 @ 22,000		120	(5.5 mins to 15,000 feet)	2 × 13 mm 1 × 20 mm
Messerschmitt Bf 110C	MF	294 @ SL 349 @ 23,000		250	(8 mins to 15,000 feet)	4 × 7.9 mm (fixed) 1 × 7.92 mm (flexible) 2 × 20 mm
Italian Aircraft						
CRDA Cant Z.501B	R	155 @ SL	1,500	500		2 or 3 × 7.7 mm
CRDA Cant Z.506B	R	195 @ SL	1,400	450		2 × 7.7 mm 1 × 12.7 mm
CRDA Cant Z.1007bis	L/R/T	280 @ 15,000	1,250	350	4,408 lb bombs or 2 torpedoes	2 × 7.7 mm 2 × 12.7 mm
Fiat CR.42	SF/FB	244 @ 6,500 266 @ 13,000	500	120	2 × 220 lb bombs (5.5 mins to 13,000 feet)	2 × 12.7 mm

Aircraft		Speed @ altitude (ft)			Armament
Macchi MC.200	SF	313 @ 15,000	100	(4.5 mins to 13,000 feet)	2 × 12.7 mm
Macchi MC.202	SF	308 @ SL 370 @ 18,000	115	(3.75 mins to 13,000 feet)	2 × 12.7 mm
Savoia Marchetti S.79	L/T/R	223 @ SL 267 @ 13,000	350	2,204 lb bombs or 2 torpedoes	1 × 7.7 mm 3 × 12.7 mm
Savoia Marchetti SM.84	T/L/R	266 @ 16,400	300	4,408 lb bombs or 2 torpedoes	4 × 12.7 mm
Japanese Aircraft					
Aichi D3A2 'Val'	D	*230 @ SL *280 @ 20,300 (267 @ 20,350)	270	1 × 551 lb bomb 2 × 132 lb bombs	2 × 7.7 mm (fixed) 1 × 7.7 mm (flexible)
Aichi E13A 'Jake'	R	*201 @ SL *222 @ 7,000 (234 @ 7,150)	250		1 × 7.7 mm
Kawanishi H6K4 'Mavis 22'	R	*198 @ SL *217 @ 6,100 (239 @ 19,685)	1,200		4 × 7.7 mm 1 × 20 mm
Kawanishi H8K2 'Emily 22'	R	*262 @ SL (270 @ 7,200) 290 @ 16,400)	1,400		4 × 7.7 mm 5 × 20 mm
Kawasaki N1K1-J 'George 11'	SF	*358 @ SL *416 @ 19,000 (362 @ 17,700)	350	(*6.1 mins to 20,000 feet)	2 × 7.7 mm 4 × 20 mm
Mitsubishi G3M2 'Nell 23'	L/T	232 @ 13,700	750	1,764 lb bombs or 1 torpedo	4 × 7.7 mm 1 × 20 mm
Mitsubishi G4M2 'Betty 22'	T/L/R	*257 @ SL *283 @ 14,000 (272 @ 15,000)	950	2,204 lb bombs or 1 torpedo	4 × 7.7 mm 2 × 20 mm
Mitsubishi J2M3 'Jack 21'	SF	*360 @ SL *417 @ 17,700 (365 @ 17,400)	250	(*5.1 mins to 20,000 feet)	2 × 13 mm 2 × 20 mm

Aircraft	Designator	Speed (mph @ ft)			Bomb/torpedo load	Armament
Mitsubishi Ki 46 'Dinah'	R (Army)	391 @ 20,000	2,250	650		1 × 7.7 mm
Nakajima B5N2 'Kate'	T/R/L	235 @ 10,000	1,240	270	1,653 lb bombs or 1 torpedo	1 × 7.7 mm
Nakajima B6N2 'Jill'	T/R	*297 @ SL *327 @ 15,100 (299 @ 16,100)	2,000	350	1 torpedo	2 × 7.7 mm
Nakajima C6N1 'Myrt'	R	*347 @ SL *396 @ 16,600 (379 @ 19,685)	2,000	600		1 × 7.92 mm
Nakajima Ki 84 'Frank'	SF (army)	*363 @ SL *427 @ 20,000 (388 @ 19,685)		200	(5.8 mins to 20,000 feet)	2 × 12.7 mm 2 × 20 mm
Yokosuka D4Y2 'Judy' 21	D/R	*325 @ SL *377 @ 19,300 (360 @ 17,225)	2,250	370	1 × 1,102 lb bomb	2 × 7.7 mm (fixed) 1 × 7.92 mm or 13 mm (flexible)
Yokosuka P1Y1 'Frances'	L/T/D	*325 @ SL *367 @ 17,000 (345 @ 19,685)	3,600	1,900	1,764 lb bombs or 1 torpedo	1 × 12.7 mm 1 × 20 mm

Japanese Navy type designators indicate the role (first letter), the number of the design in the succession of aircraft built for the role, the manufacturer (second letter), and the Mark number. Thus the B5N2 Kate was a carrier attack (torpedo) bomber, the fifth in the *Navy's* B category, built by Nakajima (N), and the second production model of the design. The B6 design was also by Najakima – Jill – but Aichi built the B7A Grace, a 340-mph torpedo-bomber which entered service in late 1944.

A = Carrier-borne fighter
B = Carrier torpedo-bomber
C = Carrier reconnaissance
D = Carrier dive-bomber
E = Catapult reconnaissance
G = Land-based bomber
H = Patrol-bomber flying-boat
J = Land-based interceptor
N = Floatplane fighter
P = Land-based attack bomber

Type designators could also be used as suffixes – D4Y1-C was a 'Judy' modified for reconnaissance duties, 'George' was a wheeled variant of the N1K1 'Rex' 300+ mph floatplane fighter.